The
Sex Secrets
of Old
England

Nigel Cawthorne has been an author for over thirty years. He has written on subjects as diverse as history, crime, sex, war and fashion. He is the author of the best-selling *Sex Lives of...* series, including (in rather dubious taste) *Sex Lives of the Popes*. Nigel Cawthorne lives in London and can usually be found in the British Library.

NIGEL CAWTHORNE

The
Sex Secrets of Old England

PIATKUS

First published in Great Britain in 2006 by Portrait, an imprint of Piatkus
Books Limited as *The Amorous Antics of Old England*
This paperback edition published in 2009 by Piatkus

A CIP catalogue record for this book
is available from the British Library

ISBN 978-0-7499-2952-7

Design and typesetting by Paul Saunders
Printed and bound in the UK by
CPI Mackays, Chatham ME5 8TD

Papers used by Piatkus are natural, renewable and recyclable
products sourced from well-managed forests and certified
in accordance with the rules of the Forest Stewardship Council.

Mixed Sources
Product group from well-managed
forests and other controlled sources
www.fsc.org Cert no. SGS-COC-004081
© 1996 Forest Stewardship Council
FSC

Piatkus
An imprint of
Little, Brown Book Group
100 Victoria Embankment
London EC4Y 0DY

An Hachette UK Company
www.hachette.co.uk

www.piatkus.co.uk

Contents

Introduction

I T MAY BE HARD to believe, but in times gone by the English were considered a particularly attractive lot – particularly when compared with the French. After visiting England, the anonymous author of *London and Paris*, published in Weimar in 1798, said, 'Here beauty in both sexes is so general that only beauty of a high order attracts attention ... such natural grace, such health, such poise.'

In his book *Romantic Love and Personal Beauty*, published in 1887, the American journalist Henry Theophilus Finck said, 'The Englishman is far and away the most beautiful animal in the world.' The English, he insisted were, both spiritually and physically, the most finely developed race in the world. This was due to Darwinian natural selection and Englishmen's romantic nature. In England, he said, a man of noble birth, 'scorning medieval puerilities, marries the girl who has won his heart, were she but a plump, rosy-cheeked peasant girl'. In contrast, on the Continent, the aristocracy had stuck to their own class and become inbred.

On top of all that the English had an addiction to outdoor sports – tennis, rowing, riding, swimming – that was responsible for their 'superior physique'. 'They are today the handsomest and most energetic race in the world,' he said.

Then there were the buses: 'English girls owe their fine physiques to long walks and travelling upstairs on the open-topped buses ... They know well, these clever girls, that their cheeks will be all the rosier, their smiles more bewitching, their eyes more sparkling after such a ride.'

The French could not compete. Nineteenth-century Parisian intellectual Hippolyte-Adolphe Taine conceded that 'generally the Englishwoman is more thoroughly beautiful and healthy than a Frenchwoman ... Out of every ten young girls one is admirable, and upon five or six a naturalist painter would look with pleasure.'

Englishwomen were also thought to be better educated, which made them more attractive, especially at an older age – even though their studies gave them lines. But it was their complexion that set English women apart: 'Many ladies have their hair decked with diamonds, and their shoulders, much exposed, have an incomparable whiteness ...'

Then there was the German art historian Gustav Friedrich Waagen, who attended a glittering ball given by the Duke of Devonshire in June 1835, and wrote,

> As though to complete the impression of a fairy world, and to add to its charm, the slender sylph-like forms of English women of rank passed in and out, for this most fashionable ball had gathered them in rare numbers. Here I encountered women like living van Dyck portraits; with the fine regular

features, the transparent, warm complexion and fair hair which he knew how to reproduce so incomparably.

The historian Johann von Archenholtz visited England the previous century and noted in 1789,

> Of all the beauties to be found in this island, none is so wonderful as the charm of the fair sex. This is so convincing that every foreigner, whatever his country, would not hesitate for an instant in awarding the prize for beauty to English women. In lovely build, in neat figure, in shape of breast, in the tender skin of the face, where the gentlest features glimmer – in all this does the English girl excel.

And it was not just the women: 'The beauty of English women may be proverbial in Europe, but the men are even better looking,' Archenholtz said.

> While there is a certain amount of justification in women being called the 'fair sex' on the Continent, in England, where the phrase is in use, it introduces a paradox that only male gallantry tolerates. For instance, if you were to walk down a line of English soldiers on parade, you would be amazed at their regular features, their beautiful eyes, their fresh complexions, the predominating oval faces, and finally at the slender disciplined build of their bodies.

He maintained that 'with the possible exception of Turkey, nowhere in Europe can so many good-looking men be found as in England'.

This masculine beauty had an astonishing effect on English womenfolk. 'Accordingly, the beauty of women, which reduces men to slaves on the Continent, does not produce anything like the same effect in England,' Archenholtz said, continuing,

> The witchery of women is rendered practically ineffective by the same magic at work in the good looks of men: and more than that – as the truth is that the effect of male beauty on women is more powerful, swifter and more lasting than that of women's beauty upon men. So it is no surprise that English girls, at least many of them, pay rather open homage to men; that they not only cast invisible nets for the hearts of men like our own lovely countrywomen, but also themselves take all the steps which have been the privilege of men in love since the beginning of the world: such as sending declarations, letters, messages by go-betweens, and all the honourable arts of courtship.

The English were not only beautiful, but were also thought to be a particularly lusty lot because of the amount of meat they ate and alcohol they drank. The average Englishman, it was reckoned, ate twice as much meat as his Continental counterpart and his consumption of liquor was titanic. When the Normans arrived at Hastings in 1066, they noted that their Anglo-Saxon opponents were drunk, even first thing in the morning. In the court of James I it was not uncommon to see ladies and gentlemen so drunk they were rolling on the floor. And it was observed that the English preferred heavy Burgundy to lighter wines – and heavy ale to light beer – beginning at breakfast. This was thought to inflame the blood.

Throughout history, the sexual shenanigans of English kings and queens have been the envy of Europe. English social life was rife with sex scandals and visitors to London were shocked by the number of prostitutes who plied their trade on the street, in the taverns, in the theatres and even in the churches. Young women who wanted to work in the sex industry flocked to London from all over Europe and prostitutes exported from England to Continental brothels were much sought after. It was only in the twentieth century that the English gained the reputation of being uptight about sex. Until then, the English were considered the Brazilians of Europe – good-looking, sexy and always at it.

CHAPTER ONE

Courting

 HEN IT CAME TO COURTING, the English were supposedly even more romantic than the Italians. In his book *Fisiologia dell' Amore* (*The Physiology of Love*), published in 1896, anthropologist Paolo Mantegazza, a correspondent of Charles Darwin, said that there was no word for 'courtship' in the Italian language. The American Henry Theophilus Finck maintained that romantic love originated in England. It was the creation of Shakespeare and the poets and novelists who followed him. This was because England was the 'first country in the world – the world of antiquity, the world of the Middle Ages, and the world of today – to remove the bars from the windows of the great women-prison, to open all doors for the unhindered entry of Cupid and to make him everywhere at home and everywhere welcome'. In *Romantic Love and Personal Beauty* of 1887, he said that the art of courtship 'even now exists in its perfection in two countries only – England and America'.

Forward women

Why did Henry Finck pick out England and America? This was partly because English women were very forward, even in the nineteenth century. Finck pointed out that there was a 'superior class of women' who had 'substituted coyness for flirtation'. Finck cited this as the reason for more romantic love in America and England, as it offered increased opportunities for courtship.

On the Continent, he maintained, women were married off directly they left school. A girl was not allowed to see a man unchaperoned, consequently 'she falls in love after marriage, and not always with her husband'. The English free-and-easy ways worked better.

While in the nineteenth century America was filling up with people of non-British origin, he noted that they all adopted the English way of making love. And how was that? Finck quoted the eighteenth-century poet and dramatist Oliver Goldsmith, saying, 'The English love with violence, and expect violent love in return.'

Seeking a spouse

The first thing a young woman had do to have a satisfactory sex life was to find a husband. In old England there were many ways she could do this. One was to take two bay leaves and sprinkle them with water on Valentine's day. That evening, she should lay them on her pillow and go to bed wearing a clean nightgown turned inside out. And before going to sleep, she should say,

Good Valentine, be kind to me,
In dreams let me my husband see.

And he would appear in her dreams.

Some girls preferred a more proactive approach. In that case, she would pluck a leaf from an even-ash and say,

This even-ash I hold in my hand
The first I meet is my true man.

She would then walk a short distance and, if she met a young man, he would be her husband. If that did not work, she would put the leaf in her glove and say,

This even-ash I hold in my glove,
The first I meet is my true love.

She would continue walking, but, if that did not work either, she would place the leaf in her bosom and say,

This even-ash I hold in my bosom
The first I meet is my husband.

Or a girl could take butterdock (*Petasites vulgaris*) seeds and scatter them in the grass half an hour before sunrise on a Friday morning, while chanting the words

I sow, I sow.
Then, my own dear,
Come here, come here
And mow, and mow.

Once this was done, her future husband would be seen mowing with a scythe some way away. In later versions, hempseed was used and the future husband was to turn up to mow it after it had sprouted.

Or the girl could wait until 28 October, stand in the middle of a room with the paring of an apple in her right hand and say:

> St Simon and Jude, on you I intrude,
> By this paring I hold to discover,
> Without any delay, to tell me this day
> The first letter of my own true lover.

After that, she should turn around three times and throw the paring over her left shoulder. When it landed, it would then form the first letter of her lover's name. But, if the paring broke in pieces or formed some indecipherable letter, the girl would remain unmarried.

St Agnes's day

However, 21 January – St Agnes's day – was also thought to be propitious. On that day, an unmarried woman should take a sprig of rosemary and one of thyme and sprinkle them with water three times. In the evening, the sprigs should be put, one each, in a pair of shoes and the shoes should be placed either side of the bed. Once the girl was in bed she should recite,

St Agnes, that's to lovers kind,
Come ease the trouble of my mind.

In 1696, the diarist John Aubrey recorded

The women have several magical secrets handed down to them by tradition for this purpose: on St Agnes' night, 21 January, take a row of pins and pull out every one, one after another, saying a Pater Noster, or 'Our Father', sticking a pin in your sleeve, and you will dream of him or her you shall marry. Or you must lie in another county, and knit the left garter about the right-legged stocking (let the other garter and stocking alone), and as you rehearse these following verses, at every comma knit a knot:

This knot I knit
To know the thing I know not yet:
That I may see
The man (woman) that shall my husband (wife) be,
How he (she) goes and what he (she) wears,
And what he (she) does, all the days and years.

The man or woman will then appear in a dream accompanied by the tools of their trade. Aubrey reported that a gentle-woman he knew had used this method and she dreamt of a man she had never seen. Two or three years later, a young preacher appeared in the pulpit and she cried out to her sister, 'This is the very face of the man I saw in my dream.'

Wedding cakes

Another virgin martyr thought to help in these matters was St Faith. On her day – 6 October – three unmarried girls were to make a cake of flour, salt, sugar and spring water, each taking an equal part in its composition. While it was baked, in a Dutch oven, silence must be strictly preserved. The cake was then cut into three equal pieces. Each girl must cut her share into nine pieces, then push each piece through a wedding ring borrowed from a woman who had been married for seven years. As the girls undressed, they ate the cake and repeated the verse,

O good St Faith, be kind tonight,
And bring to me my heart's delight;
Let me my future husband view,
And be my visions chaste and true.

The three girls then slept together in one bed, with the ring suspended over the head of it by a string. They would then dream of their future husband, if other temptations did not get in the way.

Catching a husband

In Tudor times, Midsummer's Eve was the crucial time to catch a husband. A maiden should fast, then, at midnight, lay out a clean cloth with bread, cheese and ale on it. Then she should leave the street door open and the man she was fated to marry would enter, fill the glass, drink her health, bow and depart.

This seems like a good way to catch a drunk on his way home from the pub.

Virginity tests

The book *Dreams and Moles*, published around 1780, contains a section called 'How to know whether a Female be a pure Virgin', which reads,

> Take a piece of alabaster, burn it in the fire till it may be beat to powder, then sift it through a piece of fine lawn [sheer linen]; conceal this powder till you have an opportunity to put it in her drink, when you are a merry-making; and if she drinks it, and no visible alteration appear, she hath parted with the toy you covet.

Equally, it describes how 'To know if a young Man be a chaste Batchelor or no':

> Take the seed of Cardus Benedictus [thistle], dry it that it may be beat to a powder, take the pith that grows on the shell of an oyster, and dry powder it also, and mix it with the other. Give this to the party in any liquor, and having

drunk it, if he be a true batchelor, he will oftener than usual be observed to make urine, which he will wonder at himself; but if he has lost his virginity, no such matter will happen.

Fortunately for the prospective bride, *Dreams and Moles* reveals 'How to restore a lost Maidenhead, or solder a crackt one': 'Take myrtle-berries, beat them to powder; add to this the beaten flour of cotton; being mixed, drink a little of the powder in the morning, in a glass of white wine, and you will find the effects wonderful.'

For a man who had sown his wild oats though, there was no remedy.

Lonely hearts

To find a mate in old England, you could always resort to the personal ads. These are not a new phenomenon: on 19 July 1695, the first batch of personal ads appeared in a weekly newspaper. One read, 'A gentleman, thirty years old, who says he has a very good estate, would willingly match himself to some good young gentlewoman, that has a fortune of £3,000 or thereabout' – nearly £300,000 at today's prices – 'and he will make settlement to content.'

Another said, 'A young man, twenty-five years of age, in a very good trade, and whose father will make him worth £1,000, would willingly embrace a suitable match. He has been brought up a dissenter, with his parents, and is a sober man.'

Foreign observers found it astonishing that the English should advertise for marriage partners in their newspapers.

Some even assumed the ads were a practical joke. But the idea caught on in England.

Picky personals

Personal ads allowed singletons to be very specific about their requirements. In 1777, the *Daily Advertiser* ran an ad that read,

> Wanted by a young gentleman who has just started a place of his own, a lady of eighteen to twenty-five years old, well bred and with a fortune of not less than £5,000; sound in wind and limb, 5ft 4in high without shoes on; not fat but not too thin; clean skin; sweet breath and good teeth; without conceit or affectation; not too chatty and not quarrelsome, but yet with character enough to pay back a score; generous; not over-fashionable but always decent and tidy; the sort of person who can entertain her husband's friends gaily and pleasantly, and make parties gay and attractive; who can keep his secrets so that he can open his heart to her on all occasions without restraint; who lets economy rule in the home, and can with a light heart reduce the budget if necessity requires.

Money was a prime concern. In August 1788, a London newspaper ran an ad headed ADVERTISEMENT FOR A WIFE. It read,

> Sir John Dimly, Bart., Lord of the Manor of Charleton near Worcester and of Henly Castle near Malvern Wells, wishes to make a contract of marriage with a young woman, and in the event of his death to settle on her £192,000 sterling, if

she will take him for her husband. The young woman must possess a fortune of three hundred guineas of her own. It is all one, be she virgin or widow, yes even she be pregnant by her former husband. More intimate information may be obtained from Sir John Dimly either by seeing him personally or by letter, but in the latter event postage must be paid.

Some ads were even more forthright. In August 1795, a Bristol paper carried this:

A gentleman needs a companion to journey with him towards matrimony; his intention is to depart as swiftly as possible, to leave the main roads and highways and to stroll in the paths in the woods of love. His fellow-traveller must be healthy, not too fat because that would make the journey troublesome, and to while away the hours of the marriage state, the chattier the better.

He did not reveal how long he intended to dally in the woods.

Towards the end of his life, the orientalist Edward Montagu – the son of Lady Mary Wortley Montagu and described by his biographer Henry Coates as the 'British Don Juan' – wished to have a son and heir on whom to settle his estates. By this time impotent and infirm, he advertised for a lady who was in the advanced stages of pregnancy whom he would marry. Four made the shortlist. They were then sent to Paris for Montagu's selection and each promised £200 should they be rejected. Unfortunately, Montagu was struck down with a fever in Venice and died before the final selection could be made.

Women seeking men

Women advertised, too. In the *Observer* of 22 May 1797, a young woman addressed herself directly 'To Whom it May Concern'. The ad read,

A young lady has been obliged for some years now to live secluded from the world for the pleasures of which she felt at least inclination, as her duty was to look after a sick relative. Now suddenly thrown among people, she finds that the possession of a large fortune in no way compensates her for the absence of the one person with whom she was accustomed to live. She is cut off from advantages enjoyed by others and is, in consequence, compelled to use the only means in her power, unusual as they may be, to find what she is seeking – a friend. Should a gentleman of breeding, who is not old, of good faith, pleasing, well-mannered and good family, or a lady who has such a brother or son, wish to know more of the undersigned, a few lines, should they prove agreeable, will receive careful attention: letters must be sent care of this newspaper which has the writer's address, as delicacy at first forbids any other course.

It was signed, coyly, 'Eliza'.

The advertisement appeared in the *Observer* five weeks running. Sales doubled. Eliza became the talk of London. Everyone wanted to know who she was and whether she found the man of her dreams. Naturally the response was huge and, eventually, rumours circulated that Eliza had bagged her man. One night at the opera, the attention of the author of *London and Paris* was drawn to a box where a very beautiful woman was sitting. Leaning against her chair was a tall, handsome man.

'Have a good look at that couple,' the author was told. 'That is the famous Eliza, now Mrs C., with her husband. She brought him a fortune of £70,000 and he is worth £30,000. They possess everything to make life delightful; but their greatest wealth is in themselves; they see little society and enjoy being with the boys she has borne him.'

Mr C. got lucky, but it was not unusual for prostitutes to use small ads to ensnare the unwary. They advertised themselves as young, well educated and wealthy, while the man they sought needed only a small amount of capital or a decent income. Those answering the ad would then find themselves face to face with a charming creature who would tell a tale of being mistreated by their family and friends. Thinking that they were going to enrich themselves with the fortune the woman claimed to have, these men were easy prey.

Matrimonial News

In 1870, the first paper devoted entirely to lonely-hearts ads was published in London. It was called the *Matrimonial News and Special Advertiser*. The French write Hector France called it 'the most extraordinary, the most English, the most eccentric, the most original and the most amusing journal in Great Britain'.

Most of the ads came from men unashamedly on the make. There was,

> Hubert, age twenty-six, height five feet eight, dark, is considered a handsome man, has an affectionate and loving nature, is agreeable in manner but possesses only a modest pittance. He is anxious to correspond with an elderly lady, not older then sixty however, and intends to marry immediately. She must possess the means to run a comfortable establishment.

And then there was this:

> Albert, big, dark, twenty-seven years old, without means except for his income of £80 a year, would like to make the acquaintance of a lady thirty to forty-five years old, who has the means to make a comfortable home. Photograph wanted.

Matrimonial News ran for 25 years.

Marriage Bazaar

Matrimonial clubs were set up as early as 1700. Members were supposed to aid each other to make a good match and help with the costs of the wedding. Soon after, commercial marriage agencies set up shop. The most famous was the Marriage Bazaar at 2 Dover Street, St James's. Its handbill read,

> Every visitor to Dover Street will be shown into a separate room. Whoever cannot state his wishes personally must do so in writing through a friend. Declarations must be drawn up with the greatest exactness, not only with regard to position but also to age, physical state and religion.

The fee was five guineas – £5.25 – up front, with another five due after the wedding. According to a noted critic of the time, it was a complete con.

Bundling

Away from London and its fancy balls, people did their courting horizontally, and 'bundling' was practised widely in Great Britain and across northern Europe until the nineteenth century.

In the colder months, it was not possible for a swain to woo a lass outdoors and poorer people could not afford to keep their fires going late into the evening. The cold induced the household to retire to bed early and a young lover would seek the warmth of his intended's bed. This 'courting in bed' was not done in secrecy. The young couple were expected to keep their clothes on and everything was supposed to be above board. In some cases the girl was sewn into a 'bundling sack' or a board was placed between then, so that 'outercourse' could not turn into intercourse.

The dangers of bundling

Henry VIII's fifth wife, Catherine Howard, was brought up in the household of the Dowager Duchess of Norfolk, where bundling seems to have been practised. She was 14 when she began sleeping with her music teacher Henry Manox. Both swore that full intercourse did not take place, but Catherine admitted that 'at the flattering and fair persuasions of Manox, being by a young girl, I suffered him at sundry times to handle and touch the secret parts of my body which neither became me with honesty to permit nor him to require'. When the Dowager Duchess discovered this, Manox was sacked.

Things went further when the family moved to Norfolk House in Lambeth and Catherine met her new love, Francis Dereham. They began bundling and soon were playfully calling each other 'wife' and 'husband'. Catherine's own description of what went on is explicit enough:

Francis Dereham by many persuasions procured me to his vicious purpose and obtained first to lie upon my bed with his doublet and hose and after within the bed and, finally, he lay with me naked and used me in such sort as a man doth his wife many and sundry times, but how often I know not.

Dereham and his friend, Edward Waldegrave, found a way of secretly entering the maiden's chamber at night, staying there till dawn with their respective loves, Catherine and Joan Bulmer. Dereham and Catherine would, it was reported, 'kiss and hang by their bellies as if they were two sparrows'. Love tokens were exchanged and, in the dark, there was a great deal of 'puffing and blowing'. Despite her youth, Catherine was so experienced that she knew 'how a woman might meddle with a man and yet conceive no child unless she would herself'.

These erotic games went to some extremes. Another member of the household, Katherine Tylney, later admitted that on occasions she had joined Dereham and Catherine in bed, in an intimate *ménage à trois*.

Although Catherine's behaviour was widely known, it was quickly hushed up when she caught the King's eye. To Henry, the girl was a 'blushing rose without a thorn', a 'perfect jewel of womanhood'. When he discovered the truth after they were married, Catherine was stripped of her royal title and beheaded.

Sliding knot

In his book *The Stranger in Ireland*, published in 1806, the writer John Carr recorded that a gentleman of his acquaintance was forced to leave the street door unlocked at night so that servant girls could be visited by their boyfriends – otherwise nothing would get done about the house. In Ireland, the girl stripped down to her under-petticoat, 'which is always fastened at the bottom, not infrequently, I am told, by a sliding knot,' said Carr.

English engagement

Before rings were given as a symbol of engagement, in old England a silver coin was broken in two and each half retained by the partners in the betrothal. Later a coin was just bent, which was thought to bring good luck to the union. However, following the introduction of engagement rings, men and woman made a public act of their betrothal. There would be an exchange of rings and kisses, followed by an oath: 'You swear by God and his holy saints herein and by all the saints of paradise, that you will take this woman who name is —— to wife within forty days, if Holy Church will permit.' The priest then joined their hands and said, 'And thus you affiance yourselves.' The couple answered, 'Yes, sir.'

Many couples used formal betrothal as an excuse to move in together, without waiting for the wedding ceremony. In 1622, a Puritan named Gouge condemned betrothed couples who considered themselves 'in a middle degree betwixt single persons and married persons ... yea, many take liberty after a

contract to know their spouse, as if they were married: an unwarranted and dishonest practice'. The high rate of pre-marital pregnancy bears this out.

Scottish betrothal

In old Scotland a couple could get engaged by going to a nearby stream at night, washing their hands in its waters and then joining hands across it. The poet Robert Burns was betrothed to Mary Campbell this way.

In 1869, the Reverend Charles Rogers recorded another betrothal custom in Scotland:

> The fond swain, who had resolved to make proposals, sent for the object of his affection to the village alehouse, previously informing the landlady of his intentions. The damsel, who knew the purpose of the message, busked herself in her best attire, and waited on her admirer. She was entertained with a glass of ale; then the swain proceeded with his tale of love.

The swain asked whether the girl would have him, she replied that she'd hoped he might have asked a long time ago, he said others had said she might refuse him, which she denied. Then came the formal act of betrothal: the parties licked the thumbs of their right hands, pressed them together and vowed fidelity. Anyone violating the engagement would be guilty of perjury.

Scottish courts upheld oral contracts whereby evidence was produced that the participants had licked their thumbs and pressed them together.

Engaged by Odin

In Orkney, with its Viking influence, couples called upon the Norse god Odin to witness their engagement. They would visit the Temple of Odin at Stennis by the light of the moon. On her knees, the woman would evoke the god. Then the couple would clasp hands through hole in the stone of Odin and make their pledge to wed. Until 1760, this was held to be legal by the elders of the kirk, who punished those who broke their promise to Odin.

Engagement rings

Originally an engagement ring was actually three rings held together by a small rivet, which they could easily be detached from. Together they were called a gimmal. The rings carried a design that was complete only when the three parts were together. At the engagement, one part was given to the man, one to the woman and the third to a close friend who had witness the betrothal. They would wear the three parts until the wedding, where the gimmal was recombined to make the bride's wedding ring.

Trial marriages

In parts of Yorkshire as late as 1887 a couple could enter into a trial marriage with the solemn undertaking, 'If thee tak, I tak thee' – that is, 'if you take [become pregnant] I will take you [in marriage]'. If a man pulled out after the girl conceived he would be held in contempt by his neighbours. Otherwise the couple could split and would have no trouble in finding fresh partners for another trial marriage.

In Ireland, trial marriages usually lasted a year. They were typically contracted on the Beltane festival, which falls on 1 May, and ended at the same festival the following year.

Handfasting

In many parts of England, this form of betrothal was known as 'handfasting'. The ecclesiastical courts of Durham recorded the customary form of words of the ceremony:

> After talke of agreiment the said Henry and Elizabeth wer contented ther in their presence to be handfasted, which was done by Thomas Kingston, the said Henry Smith saying … 'Here I, Henry Smith, take you, Elizabeth Frissell, to my wedded wyf etc. and thereto I plight the my trowth' … drawing handes and drinking either to other.

This betrothal was usually considered binding, although in some cases it was possible for the couple to change their minds afterwards without losing face. The betrothal could then be broken, if it was done before witnesses.

In the Lake District, 'handfasts' could be dissolved after a year and a day, if that was what both partners wanted. But, if only one party was willing, the other could sue for breach of promise in the ecclesiastical courts.

The Scottish 'handfasting' was known as 'hand in fist'. The couple entered into a one-year cohabitation agreement at a public fair. When the year was up, they would either marry or separate. In the Highlands, handfasting was also used as a form of arrangement marriage. Two chieftains would agree that the heir of one should live with the daughter of the other for one year. If the woman fell pregnant, the marriage became good in law, even though no priest had been present. Otherwise, when the year was up, the contract was considered at an end and each was free to marry or handfast with someone else.

No welshing

In Wales, in the twelfth century, a daughter was sent to go and live with a prospective husband only after a fee had been paid. If she was found to be unsuitable, she could be returned to her parents only if more money was forthcoming. The practice was so common that a woman rarely married without living with her prospective husband first.

And, until the nineteenth century, courting couples in Wales were allowed 'trial nights'. They would sleep together for one night. If everything was satisfactory, they married within a few days. If not, they parted.

CHAPTER TWO

Matrimony

N ENGLAND, WOMEN WERE more womanly and men more manly than elsewhere. Hence the permanence and happiness of married life in England, according to Hippolyte-Adolphe Taine. 'The woman in England yields herself up entirely,' he said, 'without a thought for herself. She seeks her happiness in obedience, in generosity, in service. She has only one wish – to live day by day ever more fully in the life of her husband.' Women remained loyal longer in England than elsewhere: 'Their love does not consist of tasting forbidden fruit; rather they stake their whole life on it.' How times have changed.

Marriage by purchase

Marriage by purchase originated in Anglo-Saxon times. Then, if a man had many daughters he was deemed rich, since there were many women in his household to do the cooking and cleaning, raise crops and tend livestock. So when he lost a daughter in marriage he needed compensation in the form of a *mund* or purchase price.

Under Anglo-Saxon law, if a single woman had no father she was obliged to live under the lordship of another '*mund-bora*' or protector. The dead father's place would be taken by his brother or the next male kin. If there were none, the king would take over. Once the money was paid, the *mundbora* would take the woman to her husband and hand her over with the words, 'I give thee my daughter, to be thy honour, and thy wife, to keep thy keys, and to share with thee thy bed and goods.'

A priest gave his blessing to the marriage. Then the wedding guests each had to give the couple a present. And the morning after, before he got out of bed, the groom gave his bride a valuable gift – know a '*morgaen-gife*' or morning gift – which remained her property.

A woman's price would be decided by rank, with a virgin being worth twice as much as a widow. There were four grades of widow: worth 6 shillings (30p), 12 shillings (60p), 20 shillings (£1) and 50 shillings (£2.50). So even a poor man could afford a widow if his funds did not run to a virgin.

If a man found that his wife was not in the condition that the vendor had made out – not a virgin as promised, say – he could return her and ask for his money back. On the other hand, under a later law a man had to pay a stiff fine, as well as forfeit the wedding price, if he did not marry the woman he had purchased. There were, of course, fathers who were ready to profiteer, selling the same daughter to several different men.

When King Cnut (1016–35) took over, he tried to stop the practice. He enacted a law stating that no woman could be compelled to marry against her will and that any money that changed hands as part of the marriage was to be considered a gift.

The price of love

Marriage by purchase had been rife earlier than Cnut, though: under a law of King Alfred (871–99), any man who had sex with a virgin was obliged to buy her and marry her. If her father refused his daughter's hand, the man would have to pay the bride price anyway.

Adultery was also costly. Under King Ethelred (978–1013), if a free man made free with the wife of another free man, he had to pay '*wergeld*' in compensation. And he had to purchase another wife for the wronged husband and bring her to his house. There were other punishments. Under King Edgar (959–75) an adulterer or adulteress had to live on bread and water, three days a week for seven years, while under King Cnut an adulteress had her nose and ears cut off, effectively condemning her to perpetual celibacy.

Cnut also introduced a law that prevented a widow re-marrying within a year of the death of her husband. However, Henry I (1100–35) amended the law, permitting a widow to remarry within a year provided she handed her previous husband's property over to his nearest relative.

Child marriage

Child marriage was not uncommon in old England. Records of the Bishops' Court included depositions concerning 27 cases between November 1561 and March 1565. In one case, three-year-old John Somerford married two-year-old Jane Brenton in a parish church, where the 'words of matrimony' were spoken by adults holding the children in their arms.

Ten-year-old Grace Boyes was visiting the Talbot home when she was whisked off to the church to marry 13-year-old Robert Talbot without her consent. And 10-year-old James Ballard was given two apples by a girl who enticed him 'to go to Colne and to marry her'. Eve needed only one.

As late as 1951, a girl of 14 was married by the superintendent of the Portadown Methodist Circuit, since the Act raising the age of consent to 16 in the United Kingdom did not apply to Northern Ireland.

Happy marriages

In old England it was thought that a marriage would be happy if the bride met a toad, a spider or a wolf on the way to church. But it would prove unhappy if she met a priest, a monk, a lizard, a snake, a dog or a cat.

In East Anglia, it was thought that the marriage of a woman to a man whose surname began with the same letter as hers would be unhappy. The saying ran:

To change the name, and not the letter,
It is change for the worse, not for the better.

One way to discover whether a marriage would be happy was to throw a couple of hazelnuts in the fire. If one of them exploded with a crack or shot out of the fire, the marriage would be troubled. But if they burned quietly together, it would be happy.

In the north of England, they found a way to ensure a happy marriage. Boiling water was poured on the doorstep after the married couple had left: 'keeping the doorstep warm' would bring good luck and ensure that there would be another wedding in the household shortly.

Shoes

In the parish of Avoch near Inverness in the Highlands, the best man was supposed to untie the left shoe of the groom at the door of the church and make the sign of the cross on the right side of the door with a nail or knife. To this day it is the left shoe that should be tied to the back of the married couple's

car for luck. And, at one time, if a woman got married before her older sisters, they were to dance at the reception without their shoes – otherwise they would be condemned to spinster-hood.

In terms of timing, gypsies went further. They had a custom whereby a woman was forbidden to get engaged or married before her older sister. This caused a great deal of trouble in large gypsy households and was said to be the cause of many unhappy marriages.

Marriage under the gallows

There was a popular belief in old England that if a woman who was about to be executed accepted a marriage proposal she would be reprieved. A case in point came to light in the *True Domestick Intelligence* of 21 March 1680. The paper reported that the maidservant Margaret Clark was to be hanged for setting fire to the house of her employer, Mr De La Noy, in Southwark and that 'at her execution there was a fellow who designed to marry her under the gallows (according to the ancient laudable custome), but she, being in hopes of a reprieve, seemed unwilling; but when the rope was about her neck, she cried she was willing, and then the fellow's friends disswaded him from marrying her, and so she lost her husband and life together'.

However, it seems the gesture would have been futile. The newspaper added, 'We know of no such custome allowed by law that any man's offering at the place of her execution to marry a woman condemned shall save her.'

Death or marriage

In the sixteenth century, the law in the Isle of Man stipulated that, should 'any man take a woman by constraint, for force her against her will; if she be a maid or single woman, the deemster [a Manx JP] shall give her a rope, a sword, and a ring; and she shall have her choice either to hang him with the rope, cut off his head with the sword, or marry him with the ring'.

A report on how well the law operated said,

> Every complainant has been lenient except one, who presented the rope; but relented on the prisoner being tucked up, and desired he might be let down. She then presented the ring; but the man replied that one punishment was enough for one crime: therefore he should keep the ring for some future occasion.

The bride-cup

Wine drinking in church was common practice during weddings in old England and the bride-cup was carried before the couple so that they could steel themselves during the service.

Scottish gypsies had a marriage cup or bowl made out of solid wood. It would hold two Scottish pints, or about a gallon. Once the wedding party was assembled, the priest would hand the bowl to the bride, who would urinate in it. The bridegroom would do the same. The priest then threw some earth into the bowl.

Brandy was added and the mixture was stirred using a spoon made from a ram's horn, or a ram's horn itself, which the priest carried on a piece of string around his neck. The couple then joined hands over the bowl and the priest announced, in Romany, that the couple, as man and wife, could not be separated, any more than the ingredients in the bowl could be separated.

Garters

In the north of England, young men attending a wedding vied to pluck the garter from the leg of the bride as soon as the ceremony was over. This sometimes happened when the unfortunate woman was still in front of the altar. The bride wore special ribbon garters for the occasion, which were easily detached.

The garter was also worn low on the leg to discourage overfamiliar hands. Even so, the bride was obliged to scream out and was sometimes knocked from her feet during the scrum. The victors bore the garters around the church in triumph and, afterwards, decorated their hats with them.

Bedding

After the wedding, the bride was taken to the bedchamber by the bridesmaids, who undressed her and put her to bed. The bridegroom was undressed by his friends in an adjoining room. When they were in bed, the bridesmaids took the groom's stockings and the groom's men took the bride's stockings. They then flung them at the couple. If the stocking landed on the owner's head, it was a sign that the thrower would soon marry.

Afterwards, the groom's men would retire, but the bride's mother, aunt, sister and female friends might stay on to ensure that the wedding night proceeded satisfactorily. These bedding rites continued into the eighteenth century and were even performed after the wedding of the Princess Royal, daughter of George II, to the Prince of Orange in 1733.

First-footing

Evenus III (12–5 BC), the 16th king of Scotland, enacted a law that gave the king the right to avail himself of the first night after marriage of any nobleman's daughter, while the noblemen were allowed the same privilege with the daughters of their tenants and vassals.

On top of that, all the wives and daughters of his subjects should be held in common to the king and all his nobles. The wife of Malcolm III (AD 1058–93), Queen – later Saint – Margaret insisted that he ban the practice, introducing a bridal tax instead.

Elsewhere, though, no doubt feudal lords took advantage, the *just primae noctis* or *droit du seigneur* was never established in civil law.

Fleet weddings

Marriage in old England was a bit of a mess. Although the church had established its jurisdiction in Anglo-Saxon times, a number of religious houses remained outside the control of the church authorities and were happy to marry all-comers for a fee, without making too many enquiries into their background. Henry VIII's Dissolution of the Monasteries in 1540 did little to help the situation.

In spite of laws in the sixteenth and seventeenth centuries concerning, among other things, the reading of banns, the requirement that a couple should be married in a church where one of them lived, that no church could claim to be outside ecclesiastical authority and that clergymen could allow other priests to hold clandestine ceremonies in their churches and chapels, one place that continued to conduct marriages was Fleet prison. It was privately owned and only the Crown had right of visitation.

The prison wardens quickly realised that they could make a handsome profit if they allowed ministers imprisoned there for debt or more serious crimes to perform marriages, while themselves keeping the authorities out.

There were attempts made to regulate marriage in the Fleet but, in 1702, the exemption from ecclesiastical visitation was upheld, not just for the prison, but also the 'Rules' around it, where debtors who could not fit into the overcrowded prison were housed under prison rules. Chapels sprang up in the surrounding pubs, which did roaring trade. Not only did they marry people who would have been illeligible to marry elsewhere, but they would also doctor documents so that any child accidentally born before the marriage would become legitimate. In the 1720s, over 4,000 Fleet weddings were being performed each year.

The very fact that they were Fleet weddings was hidden by the certificate, which described the venue as St Bride's, Fleet Street, or some other prestigious-sounding venue.

Drunken clergymen

In 1735, a woman wrote to the *Gentleman's Magazine* complaining about the number of marriages conducted in the Fleet 'by a crowd of drunken clergymen in black coats who purported to be "clerks" and "registrars to the Fleet", who walked up and down Ludgate Hill and persuaded those in ale houses and gin shops to marriage, thereby keeping them on the Sabbath from attendance at church'.

Grubby touts – know as plyers – would accost prospective clients on the street, ready to marry a couple for a twist of tobacco or a glass of gin. This presented a grand opportunity for adventurers of either sex, but particularly for women who were mired in debt. Marriage meant that their debts passed to their new husband.

By the 1740s, 6,500 weddings were taking place in the Fleet a year – over half the marriages in London. Another thousand clandestine weddings were taking place illegally in the Mayfair Chapel in Curzon Street. The chaplain there, Alexander Keith, was prosecuted and eventually ended up in the Fleet on a writ of excommunication for his matrimonial offences. But even this did not put him out of business. Marriages continued in Mayfair, conducted by parsons from the Fleet and with certificates signed by Keith.

The whole thing came to an end with Lord Hardwicke's Act of 1753, outlawing clandestine marriages, but that did not stop the trade. An advertisement that year promised marriages in the ancient Royal Chapel of St John the Baptist at the Savoy Palace, with great secrecy.

Gretna Green

With the passing of Hardwicke's Act in 1754 those wishing to marry in haste found that all they had to go to Scotland, where the Act did not apply. Under Scottish law a couple had only to declare their wish to get married before witnesses. Thus Gretna Green, just north of the River Sark, which marks the border between England and Scotland, came into its own.

An Englishman who married there in 1790 wrote of a 'cement master' who performed ceremonies. After he had been found – in a tavern – and brought to the couple, he demanded the equivalent of £31.50 – over £2,500 today – but was talked down to 10 guineas (£10.50).

When the bridegroom asked about the signatures of witnesses, the dubious 'official' said, 'This moment you shall have a couple of them', and wrote two strange names.

'And we travelled back to England a properly married couple,' wrote the groom.

The advent of the railway boosted the marriage business in Gretna, but then, in 1856, the law in Scotland was changed and required one of the partners to the marriage to reside in Scotland for 21 days before the ceremony. After 1940, couples

had to be married by a minister or registrar. However, runaway couples kept coming because, in Scotland, you could marry at 16 without parental consent, while in England you had to wait until 21. But in 1969, the age of marriage without parental consent was changed to 18 throughout the United Kingdom and the legal incentive to marry in Gretna vanished.

An unfortunate elopement

In 1777, Dorothea Kinsman ran off with Tenduci, her singing Italian teacher, who was a eunuch. Against all odds, they lived together in Naples for seven years until she found something was missing from her marriage. Then in 1784, she broke her silence and wrote home to her father to say that she was upset and realised that a union with a eunuch was not 'a holy bond in the sight of heaven'.

Her father sent money and she fled back to Britain, where she petitioned for an annulment. Her deposition explained how Siena-born Tenduci had been totally castrated. They had been secretly married by a Catholic priest, on their arrival in Italy, she posed as his pupil. There was a law in Italy, she said, that would condemn to the gallows a eunuch who married.

An English court proclaimed the marriage null and void, and ordered Tenduci to pay costs. But there is a footnote to this story. Although Tenduci had had his testicles removed, he later proved his virility with a number of women in Paris. Nor had he lost his balls completely. An Irish officer was present one day when Tenduci was dressing. Seeing him take a small red velvet bag from his pocket, the officer asked whether it contained sacred relics from Rome.

'No,' said Tenduci. 'Those are my testicles. I keep them with me in this bag ever since they were cut off.'

An Elizabethan annulment

In 1561, a Devonian named John Bury had his marriage annulled due to impotence. Before the wedding a horse had kicked him in the groin, deforming his testicles. But he married again and his second wife gave birth to a son.

When Bury died in 1599, the child stood to inherit. But probate was contested by the next in line, a Mr Webber. He argued that the boy was a bastard. If Bury was impotent, the boy could not be his son, so could not inherit. And if the boy was his son and Bury was not impotent, the second marriage was unlawful, because the first was still valid. So the boy was a bastard and could not inherit.

After a great deal of legal wrangling, it was decided that the child could inherit on the grounds that any challenge to Bury's second marriage had to be made during his lifetime and that English common law regards any progeny of a valid marriage legitimate, whoever the father was.

CHAPTER THREE

Seduction

 EDUCTION WAS AS MUCH a part of the amorous antics of old England as courtship and marriage – and there was a lot of it about. One concerned member told the Guardian Society for the Preservation of Public Morals in 1818 that 'the seduction of unmarried females is more practised, and more openly practised, in Great Britain, than any other civilised state in the world' and that 'it has spread through every rank of society'.

Damaged goods

In old England it was possible to bring a civil action for damages for 'seduction'. The eighteenth-century radical politician and libertine John Wilkes was worried about falling foul of the law if he took a certain young lady from her father into his home, so he consulted the top barrister, king's counsel and speaker of the House of Commons Sir Fletcher Norton.

Norton advised him to take the girl on as a servant and give her double wages. The extra money, Norton said, would 'denote that something more than common services were expected to be performed by her'. Wilkes took this advice, employed the girl as a chamber maid for the princely sum of £20 a year and slept with her – all the while 'swearing by his goddess Venus, that the name of a lawyer was but another for scoundrel'.

Love powder

If you wished to seduce, you could, of course, always slip something into a victim's drink. The *circa* 1780 book *Dreams and Moles* contained a section that told you how 'To make an excellent Love Powder':

> Take nettle-feed and juniper-berries, dry and beat them to powder; then burn in the fire the claw of a crab, that it may also be powdered; mix them, and giveth the party as much as will lie on a silver penny in any liquor, and it will cause strange effects without harm; by which a husband or wife thro' good management, may be obtained.

But there were laws against the use of such concoctions. Lady Elizabeth Grey was tried before Parliament, accused by Richard III of having lured Edward IV into marriage with a love potion.

The irresistible strip

Oscar Wilde's mother, Jane ('Speranza'), Lady Wilde, published *Ancient Cures, Charms, and Usages of Ireland* in 1890, which recorded the use of a love philtre called the 'dead strip'. She wrote,

Girls have been known to go to the graveyard at night, exhume a corpse that has been nine days buried, and tear down a strip of the skin from head to foot; this they manage to tie around the leg or arm of the man they love while he sleeps, taking care to remove it before his awaking. And so long as the girl keeps this strip of skin in her possession, secretly hidden from all eyes, so long will she retain the man's love.

Seduced by the Devil

In the fifteenth century, a young woman in Scotland had refused marriage proposals from the sons of several noble houses. But when a handsome young man turned up she could not resist and admitted him to her chamber – though she had no idea who he was and where he came from.

The resulting amorous activity aroused the rest of the household, who turned up – or so it is said – with torches to find her in the clutches of a monster, 'so revolving it exceeded human imagination'. A priest arrived and began reading the

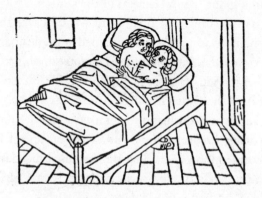

Gospel of St John. The demon then let out a terrible cry and fled, taking the roof off the chamber as he went and setting the furniture on fire. Three days later, the woman gave birth to a monster. It was burned to protect the reputation of the family.

Man make-up

To win a lover it is important to make the best of your appearance. The ancient Celtic inhabitants of the British Isles used hair lotion, rouge and hair dye. Tweezers have been found in the graves of Anglo-Saxon women, which were thought to have been used to pluck superfluous hair. They also dyed their hair. But after the Danish invasion it was principally men who wore cosmetics.

Make-up remained out of fashion for women for centuries. A German visitor to England in the eighteenth century said, 'English women rely on their natural beauty so much that they despise artificial aid. Only a few *filles de joie* put on rouge. Many never put powder on their hair, even on the most festive occasions. Cleanliness, which is carefully attended to, increases immeasurably the natural charms of the fair sex.'

This is misleading. The Bristol and Windsor soap they used often came in 'washballs' that contained white lead and mercury to whiten the skin, often in dangerous amounts.

Another foreign observer, plainly mixing in different circles, said that English women had perfected the art of applying face powder and rouge during the eighteenth century. Perfumes came in from France, Italy, Spain, Portugal and Turkey. A Danish cosmetic was also doing the rounds, which contained various beauty waters, along with vinegar, borax, eggs, bread and the wings and heads of doves, and was supposed to give a woman of 50 the complexion of a 20-year-old.

Powder tax

The fashion for powdering the hair had begun in the sixteenth century, but rose to its height in the eighteenth. Then, in June 1795, a punitive tax was slapped on powder. Some 300,000 people paid a guinea – £1.05, or £70 at today's prices – for the right to use powder for a year.

Some immediately gave it up. Others took to having their dogs and horses powdered as this did not attract the tax. However, the tax soon had its desired effect, forcing powder out of fashion. In September 1795, the Duke of Bedford hosted a party at Woburn Abbey to ceremoniously renounce powder. Numerous prominent men and Members of Parliament attended.

Gingered up

In Georgian times oysters, lobster, turtle, fish, eggs, artichokes, celery, onions, cocoa, ginger, pepper, apricots, strawberries, peaches, buckwheat, mushrooms and truffles were all used as aphrodisiacs. George IV rated the aphrodisiac properties of truffles so highly that his ambassadors in Italy were ordered to seek out the best they could find and send them to the royal kitchens by special courier.

While ginger was taken internally as an aphrodisiac, it was also applied externally as a stimulant. In John Campbell's *The Amatory Experiences of a Surgeon*, published in London in 1881, the male protagonist seduces two young women by touching them with hands rubbed with ginger.

A brief history of kissing

Kissing is obviously an important part of any seduction and the origins of English osculation were outlined in an article that appeared in the *St James Magazine* in 1871:

> It is quite certain that the custom of kissing was brought to England from Friesland, as St Pierius Wensemius, historiographer to their High Mightinesses of the states of Friesland, in his *Chronicle*, 1622, tells us that the pleasant practice of kissing was utterly 'unpractised and unknown in England until the fair Princess Romix (Rowena), the daughter of King Hengist of Friesland, pressed the beaker with her lips, and saluted the amorous Vortigen with a *kusjen'* (little kiss).

After that, kissing caught on in a big way. Visiting England in 1499, the scholar Erasmus wrote home,

> If you go any place (in Britain) you are received with a kiss by all; if you depart on a journey, you are dismissed with a kiss; you return, kisses are exchanged … wherever you move, nothing but kisses. And if you, Faustus, had but once tasted them – how soft they are, how fragrant! On my honour, you would wish not to reside here for ten years only, but for life.

And Erasmus was a monk. Not that being a man of the cloth mattered. At that time the priest who performed a wedding ceremony was rewarded with a kiss, not just from the bride, but also all the bridesmaids – making a career in the ministry extremely popular.

Indeed, the English got so good at kissing that they were soon exporting the art. At the court of notoriously promiscuous Queen Christina of Sweden, Cromwell's ambassador extraordinaire Bulstrode Whitelocke was asked to teach the ladies 'the English mode of salutation; which, after some pretty defences, their lips obeyed, and Whitelocke most readily'. The queen was so impressed with Whitelocke's smooching that Sweden signed a treaty of amity with England, which is still in force to this day.

Kissing did not fare so well back home under the Puritans, though. John Bunyan, author of *The Pilgrim's Progress*, did not approve of all this kissing. Why is it, he enquired, when it comes to kissing women that men only 'salute the most handsome and let the ill-favoured alone'? Well, if you have to ask …

Then, with the Restoration in 1660, the English were again showing the world how kissing should be done. That year Samuel Pepys had seen some Portuguese ladies in London. 'I find nothing in them that is pleasing; and I see they have learnt to kiss,' he said, 'and I do believe will soon forget the reclusive practice of their own country.'

Gently does it

So how should we kiss? In *Romantic Love and Personal Beauty* Henry Theophilus Finck gave some advice.

'Kissing comes by instinct, and yet it is an art which few understand properly,' he said. 'A lover should not hold his bride by the ears in kissing her, as appears to have been customary in Scotch weddings of the last century. A more graceful way, as quite as effective in preventing the bride from "getting away", is to put your right arm round her neck, your fingers under her chin, raise the chin, and then gently but firmly press your lips on hers. After a few repetitions she will find out it doesn't hurt, and will become as gentle as a lamb.'

Finck also pointed out that 'the word adoration is derived from kissing. It means literally to apply the mouth. Therefore girls should beware of philologists who may ask them with seemingly harmless intent, "May I adore you?" '

He did, however, disagree with the poet and journalist Leigh Hunt, who said stolen kisses are the sweetest. According to Finck, for 'a kiss to be a kiss it has to be mutual, voluntary, simultaneous. "This kiss snatched hastily from the sidelong maid" is not worth having. A stolen kiss is only half a kiss.'

CHAPTER FOUR

Criminal Conversation

N THE EIGHTEENTH AND nineteenth centuries adultery was described as *criminal conversation*, and a husband could seek damages in court from a man who had seduced his wife. However, a wife could not sue another woman for criminal conversation with her husband. The legal opinion was: 'Forgiveness on the part of a wife, especially with a large family, in the hopes of reclaiming her husband is meritorious; while a similar forgiveness on the part of the husband would be degrading and dishonourable.'

All the news unfit to print

To satisfy the public appetite for the sordid details of criminal-conversation cases the press coverage was collected in the twelve volumes of the *Crim.-Con. Biography: or celebrated trials in the Ecclesiastical and Civil Courts for Adultery and other Crimes connected with Incontinency, from the Period of Henry the Eighth to the Present Time by Francis Plowden, Esq., of Doctors' Common*, published in London in 1789.

This vast library of near-pornographic material is tastefully illustrated with pictures of Mrs Harris offering her bosom to her beloved clergyman, Mrs Draper on the knee of her clerk, Mrs Abergavenny showing her huge bosom to Sir Lyddel, with the caption 'You are as necessary to me as the air I breathe', and Milady Grosvenor caught in bed with the Duke of Cumberland while her husband is taking his revenge with a serving girl. Reprinted in 1830, it lost the illustrations and was cut down to two volumes.

There was even a newspaper that specialised in publishing full accounts of juicy divorce cases. Officially entitled the *Diurnal Register of the Treates* [sic] *and Follics of the Present Day* – known informally as the *Crim.-Con. Gazette* – it ran to eighteen issues between 20 November 1830 and 30 April 1831. It was illustrated and came to an end when its contents were ruled to be obscene.

Then along came the *Crim.-Con. Gazette* in August 1838, which published 70 issues until it changed its name to the *Bon Ton Gazette* in January 1840.

Numerous other crim.-con. titles were published, delivering the salacious details of individual cases. Then, in 1890, *Crim.-Con: Actions and trials and other proceedings relating to marriage before the passing of the present Divorce Act* – which finally abolished the concept of criminal conversation – was published.

There is, of course, a great deal of crossover between these sources.

Block and tackle

Sensational sex cases were always much more fun when they involved the upper classes. The earliest case to be reported in the *Crim.-Con* of 1890 was the trial of Mervin Tuchet, Lord Audley, Earl of Castlehaven, on 25 April 1631. It seems Lord Audley liked to force his wife to have sex with footmen, while his lordship used the man from behind.

This behaviour began shortly after they were married when the earl summoned a footman named Amptil to their marriage bed. The countess said that the earl spoke obscenely to her, telling her that her body was his property to dispose of how he wished. He then ordered her to let Amptil enjoy her in the same way he, as her husband, had done. He urged her to sleep with other men and relished the idea that she would give birth to a son as a result. She said she was forced to obey.

On another occasion, he called the servant into their bedroom, ogled his private parts and forced her to do the same. With the aid of oil, the earl sodomised her and he did the same with his footmen. The footmen and other witnesses confirmed much of what the countess said. The earl held her down while a servant named Giles Broadway raped her. Afterwards the countess tried to kill herself, but Broadway wrested the knife from her hand.

The earl was found guilty of rape by a unanimous vote of his peers. And he was convicted on two counts of sodomy by a vote of 15 to 12. The sentence was death by hanging, but this was commuted to beheading. For a man of his class, the swift stroke of an axe was considered a more merciful and fitting end. He was executed on Tower Hill on 14 May 1631.

Evidence of adultery

Witnesses did not hold back when it came to the details in criminal-conversation cases. One Mrs Harris had told her housemaid to hang fresh curtains around her bed, as she was expecting her husband. But Reverend John Craven turned up instead. Various maids, women friends and the lady's young sister kept watch in the corridor outside all night. They heard the bed creak and the housemaid said she had found stains in the bed, the same 'as [Queen Caroline's maid] Barbara Kreutz saw in that of the unfortunate queen of England' – wife of George IV.

A footman testified that he had seen his mistress and her lover in a field 'in a very extraordinary situation'. When the judge asked him to describe the position, the footman got down on all fours in the courtroom.

A bishop testified that his wife had seduced a young man she had brought to the house under the pretext that he was going to marry their daughter. However, the daughter told him that her mother and the pretended fiancé spent their nights together. So he hid himself and overheard kisses being exchanged. When silence fell, he, his daughter and a footman broke down their door and saw, by the light of the lamps they were carrying, 'the amorous couple naked in the same bed'.

When a witness was less than forthcoming, magistrates would go to great lengths to wheedle out the most obscene details. A French commentator described judges in criminal-conversation trials as the worst pornographers in the country.

Charms to preserve virtue

In old England, women wore charms around their necks to preserve their virtue. But that also meant that both charm and virtue could be dispensed with easily. On 6 March 1804, Lock-hart and Lauden Gordon appeared at Bow Street Magistrates' Court, charged with abducting Mrs Rachael Fanny Antonia Lee, the illegitimate daughter of Lord Despenser. But in cross-examination, Mrs Lee admitted that, when the chaise they were carrying her off in reached Uxbridge, 'she found it useless to make further resistance, and tearing from her breast a gold locket and a camphire bag, she exclaimed, "the charm that has pre-served my virtue hitherto is dissolved"'. Camphor was reputed to be an antaphrodisiac. She threw it away and 'now welcomed pleasure'.

At an inn in Tetsworth that night, when she was ready for bed, Mrs Lee asked the chambermaid 'to tell her "husband" that he might come to bed in ten minutes'. The trial was stopped at this point and Lockhart and Lauden Gordon were acquitted. However, a hostile mob formed and Mrs Lee had to stay locked in the yard of the court until it dispersed.

The indelicate investigation

The most famous crim.-con. case of the nineteenth century was brought against Princess Caroline of Brunswick-Lüneburg by her husband the prince regent, later George IV. It resulted in 52 days of the salacious testimony before the House of Lords in 1820s. While the British public relished every sordid detail, observers on the Continent were shocked. The Danish writer Georg Brandes called it an 'incredible scandal which flowed like a sewer from the floor of the House of Lords and sank the lustre of the Crown and the fair name of the reigning family in a sea of mud'.

As Prince of Wales, George had had numerous affairs and had lived with Catholic divorcee Mrs Maria Fitzherbert, who bore him 10 children. But, when his profligacy resulted in financial difficulties, his father George III promised to help him out – provided he marry a foreign princess and produce an heir. Princess Caroline of Brunswick was selected. The marriage was a disaster from the beginning: George hiccupped throughout the wedding ceremony and that night got so drunk that he slept with his head in the fireplace. He did his duty, though, the following morning. To everyone's surprise, Caroline gave birth to a daughter, Princess Charlotte, nine months later.

To all intents and purposes the marriage was over. Caroline had moved to Blackheath. There, according to Lady Hester

Stanhope, she had become 'a downright whore'. She was frequently 'closeted with young men'. In her front room, she had a Chinese clockwork figure that, when you wound it up, made gross sexual movements and she liked to dance around showing off a good deal of her body.

Her partner in crime was Lady Douglas, who had been shunned by polite society for having an affair with her husband's commanding officer, Sir Sidney Smith. Not only did Lady Douglas take lovers whenever she felt like it, she also slept with Caroline.

When the two of them fell out, Caroline sent Lady Douglas's husband, Sir John Douglas, an obscene drawing showing his wife making love to Sir Sidney Smith. Rumours flew that a four-year-old boy in their circle named William Austin was Caroline's son by Prince Louis Ferdinand of Prussia. This caused such a scandal that the Privy Council set up a committee to look into the Princess of Wales's behaviour. It was called the 'Delicate Investigation'.

The commission investigated every sordid detail of the goings-on in Blackheath. Of particular public interest was her relationship with Captain Manby, a naval officer who was a frequent visitor. However, on the substantive charge, that she had a love child, Caroline was exonerated and Lady Douglas, who has started the rumour, was found guilty of perjury.

In 1814, Caroline left England and started a scandalous progress across Europe. She began by dancing topless at a ball in Geneva given in her honour. In Naples, she had an affair with Napoleon's brother-in-law King Joachim. In Milan, she took up with Bartolomeo Pergami – known as Bergami in England – a former quartermaster in Napoleon's Italian army. They travelled around Europe, North Africa and the Middle East together as man and wife, before setting up home in Como.

With her own reputation in tatters, Caroline tried to ruin her daughter's too. Charlotte had been strictly brought up by her maiden aunts in Windsor. But, when she visited her mother, Caroline locked the young virgin in a room with Captain Hesse, who was said to be the illegitimate son of the Duke of York, who was her uncle, and one of Caroline's own lovers.

In 1820, George III died and the prince regent came to the throne as George IV. Caroline was now seen as a threat, a ready focus for public animosity towards the spendthrift new king. George IV offered her £50,000 a year if she promised to remain abroad. But Caroline now considered herself Queen of England and was determined to be crowned in Westminster Abbey alongside her husband.

She returned to England and was immediately arrested and arraigned before the House of Lords for 'a most unbecoming and degrading intimacy with a foreigner of low station' – Pergami. A Bill of Pains and Penalties was drawn up, which, George hoped, would dissolve their marriage on the grounds of adultery. The matter was debated in lascivious detail by the House of Lords from 19 August to 10 November 1820. The newspapers lapped it up.

Witnesses were called, including servants from Caroline's own household. They said they had seen Caroline and Pergami naked together. Pergami had been seen caressing Caroline's breasts and her inner thigh. They had slept together. He was frequently seen naked, or semi-naked in her bedroom and was present when she took a bath. Then there were those telltale stains. It seemed an open-and-shut case.

However, George IV had not taken into account the power of public opinion. Naturally, the public had lapped up every juicy detail of the case. But people also knew what the King had been up to and widely believed that what was sauce for the goose was sauce for the gander. The Duke of Wellington was stopped by a mob in London, who shouted, 'God save the Queen.'

'Well, gentlemen, since you will have it so,' said the Iron Duke, 'God save the Queen – and may all your wives be like her.'

Caroline herself found that she was cheered by crowds when she travelled daily from her new home in Brandenburg House, Hammersmith, to the Houses of Parliament. The crowds of her supporters there were so huge that a stout timber fence had to be built around the House of Lords. She frequently dozed off during the proceedings and, when she was asked whether had ever committed adultery, she said only when she slept with 'Mrs Fitzherbert's husband'.

In the end, the Bill was passed with a majority of just nine.

But the matter had become a *cause célèbre*. To save further embarrassment, the government discreetly dropped it, rather than take it forward to the House of Commons.

One contemporary satirist wrote:

Most gracious Queen we thee implore
To go away and sin no more;
Or if that effort be too great
Go away at any rate.

But she wouldn't. At the coronation on 19 July 1821, Queen Caroline turned up at Westminster Abbey uninvited and the doors were slammed in her face. She fell ill and died 19 days later.

Love letters

In old England, far from being dainty evocations of one's most tender feelings, love letters were often explicitly sexual. Letters from the famous actor Edmund Kean to Mrs Robert Albion Cox were read out in open court during a crim.-con. trial in 1825. They were so inflammatory that Kean was ordered to pay damages of £800 – worth £45,000 today – to Mr Cox, a shareholder in the Drury Lane Theatre, where Kean had been resident during his seven-year clandestine affair with Cox's wife.

Worse still was the correspondence between a 45-year-old mother, Lady Cavendish, and the young Count de la Rochefoucauld. Rochefoucauld's letters were so erotic that 12 of them occupy the last 26 pages of the fourth volume of the pornographic classic *Romance of Lust*, published in 1876, which is still confined to the Private Case in the British Library and kept in the strong room there.

When counsel for Lord Cavendish produced them, he said that, in his opinion, they were too scandalous to be read out in open court. The judge had a look at one or two and told the court, 'I entirely agree with my learned friend. I shall take them home and refer to them in my summing up.'

In them, Rochefoucauld said that Lady Cavendish had picked 'the flower of his virginity'. He talked of the joys of cunnilingus, fellatio, drinking urine, eating faeces and sharing all the delicacies of each other's body.

He talked of introducing naked young serving girls to their lovemaking who would perform cunnilingus on Lady Cavendish and 'violate you with her breasts ... filling your womb with her milk to excite your senses'. He wrote of even more 'debased' practices, but his letters are much too explicit to be reproduced here. God knows what Lady Cavendish's were like. They have been lost. But, in his letters, Rochefoucauld repeatedly said that Lady Cavendish's replies were even hotter.

Negligence

In a criminal-conversation case, if a husband had been in any way neglectful, negligent or complicit, the wife and seducer escaped all punishment.

In one case an old colonel brought a young subaltern home for dinner, who took a fancy to the colonel's wife. After dinner while the colonel sat at table finishing the wine, the subaltern had his wife on the sofa in the next room. It was considered that the colonel had not taken care to protect his wife, which was deemed to be the duty of all English husbands. He won the crim.-con. case, but was awarded just one shilling – 5p – damages.

In a more extreme case, a certain lord was so proud of his wife's body, which he compared to the *Venus de Medici* now in the Uffizi, that he decided to show his wife naked to his friends while she was having a bath. The lord even let one of the friends – who himself, the lord said, was married to a 'callipygian Venus', that is one with round buttocks – climb up on his shoulders for a better view. The friend became so enflamed by what he had seen, he became determined to seduce the lady and eventually succeeded. When the husband brought action against his friend for criminal conversation, the jury found against him and he himself was punished.

Dirty linen

The nineteenth century drew to a close with another celebrated aristocratic crim.-con. case and aired all sorts of dirty linen in public. In 1884, Lady Colin Campbell had won a suit against her husband for cruelty and the judge ordered a separation. Lord Campbell sued for divorce, naming the Duke of Marlborough, Colonel Butler, Captain Shaw and Dr Bird as co-respondents. Lady Campbell countersued, naming her maid, Mary Watson. The case opened at the Law Courts on 26 November 1886.

Evidence was given that Dr Bird had been present at a miscarriage, or perhaps an abortion, which removed the evidence of his activities. Mary Watson was seen sitting on Lord Campbell's bed with her arms around him. Another of Lady Campbell's maids, Rosa Baer, said that she had seen her ladyship committing adultery with Lord Blandford. Lord Campbell's manservant O'Neil had also seen, through a keyhole, Lady Campbell lying on the floor with Captain Shaw.

A maid named Eliza Wright testified that Lady Campbell had had syphilis before her marriage. Lord Campbell had been treated for the condition before the wedding and Lady Campbell insisted that she had contracted the disease only after her marriage and that she had caught it from her husband.

Doctors gave conflicting testimony about the miscarriage and Lady Campbell's physical ability when it came to sexual intercourse. And two esteemed medical men claimed they had examined Mary Watson and she was still a virgin. All this was presented in open court in front of such noted personages as the Duke of Argyll and the Marquis of Lorne, who was the son-in-law of Queen Victoria.

In the end, the jury acquitted all the defendants and Lord Campbell was ordered to pay £15,000 costs – £1 million in today's money.

Afterwards, in the House of Lords, Lord Lyndhurst complained that this kind of case was 'a disgrace to our legal practice', that 'no [other] European country would tolerate it' and that Continental lawyers he had talked to condemned the English legal system for allowing it. In his speech, Lyndhurst characterised the proceedings by quoting direct from the pages of *Crim.-Con.* describing the publicity surrounding the cases as 'scandalous and improper' and the evidence of servants and young ladies-maids as 'no less than a kind of prostitution'.

Soon afterwards, the Divorce Act was passed and the golden age of English criminal conversation was over.

CHAPTER FIVE

Other Arrangements

N London in Elizabethan times it was not necessarily a disgrace to be cuckolded. In fact, it was celebrated. About three miles east of St Paul's on the Surrey shore, there was Cuckold's Haven or Cuckold's Point, which was marked by a pole with a cuckold's horns on top. According to the Elizabethan poet Nicholas Breton, it had been raised to honour Lady Fortune, the subversive spirit of marriage and cuckoldry. The reason was that London was growing fast. New trade routes were opening up, making a great many wealthy men, and they took trophy wives. These often slipped from their grasp. Being a cuckold was part of the price a man paid for being rich.

No shame

Foreign observers were surprised that English cuckolds even advertised the fact. When a ship's captain found his wife in a compromising situation with one of his sailors, he had her stripped naked and put astride a mast alongside her lover. This then was bedecked with streamers and carried around the streets of east London on the shoulders of his other crewmen. It was followed by a band and a crowd of onlookers.

In England, it was noted, the disgrace belonged not to the cuckolded husband but to his wife's lover. Consequently, it was considered ridiculous for the wronged husband to challenge his rival to a duel, as happened in other countries.

Making an exhibition

During a trip to London, a nobleman from the countryside suspected his wife was having an affair. So he told her that he was going on an excursion. That night he returned to find her in bed with an army officer. He and his men tied them to the bedposts, then he put the adulterous couple on exhibition to his friends. The friends told other friends, who also turned up to view the couple's plight. They were kept on display for four days and fed nothing but bread and water.

Wife selling

There was another way to deal with an adulterous or otherwise unsatisfactory wife: sell her. In 1302, John de Camoys signed a deed of transfer by which he 'delivered and yielded up' both his wife Margaret and her goods and chattels to Sir William de Paynel.

In 1553, clergyman Thomas Snowdel, also known as Parson Chicken, sold his wife to a butcher after Mary I announced that all priests who had married during the brief period of Protestantism preceding her reign should be turned out of their livings.

The shilling wife

In the eighteenth century the selling of wives became commonplace. On 31 August 1773, three men and three women went to the Bell Inn in Edgbaston Street, Birmingham, and made the following entry in the toll book kept there: 'Samuel Whitehouse, of the parish of Willenhall, in the county of Stafford, this day sold his wife, Mary Whitehouse, in open market, to Thomas Griffiths, of Birmingham, value one shilling. To take her with all faults.' And a man in Nottingham sold his wife for a shilling (5p) to a blacksmith just three weeks after the wedding.

Livestock prices

There were fears that inflation was on the horizon. *The Times* of 22 July 1797 said sarcastically,

> By some mistake or omission, in the report of Smithfield market, we have not learned the average price of wives for

the week. The increasing value of the fair sex is esteemed by several eminent writers the certain criterion of increasing civilisation. Smithfield has, on this ground, strong pretensions to refined improvement, as the price of wives has risen in that market from half a guinea [£42 today] to three guineas and a half [£294].

This was no joke. On 12 April 1817, the French travel writer Victor Joseph Étienne de Jouy had seen a man struggling to put a rope around the neck of a pretty young woman in Smithfield Cattle Market in front of a huge crowd. She resisted and caused such a commotion that they were both arrested. The man explained to the magistrate that he was selling his wife because she had been unfaithful. She did not deny the charge. As there was no law against selling a wife, the magistrate could do nothing except deplore their conduct and bind them over to keep the peace. A wife was, after all, a man's property, and it was perfectly legal for a man to sell his own property.

But there could be compensations. If the buyer was of a romantic bent, a church wedding would occur after the sale. In earlier times, a lord who seduced the wife of a vassal could make amends this way. By buying the woman he could marry her and compensate the wronged husband.

According to the periodical *All the Year Round* the Annual Register for 1832 told of Joseph Thomson, a farmer, who agreed to separate from his wife after a brief married life of three years. So he put her up for auction in Carlisle and in his sales pitch spoke of her as a 'born serpent' and his 'tormentor'. But then he gave some of her good points: she could read novels and milk cows, make butter and scold the maid, and, while she couldn't make rum, gin or whisky, she was 'a good judge of the quality from long experience of tasting them'.

So he offered her for 50 shillings – £2.50 or £160 today.

However, Thomson seems to have oversold his wife's faults. After an hour, she was knocked down to Henry Mears for 20 shillings and a Newfoundland dog, 'and the parties separated, being mutually pleased with their bargain'.

Life's a lottery

Simple barter was employed. *Gentleman's Magazine* said that in 1764 a Norfolk farmer offered to exchange his wife for an ox, the only stipulation being that he got to pick the ox for himself – presumably he wanted a pretty one. And the *Public Advertiser* of 19 September 1768 said, 'On Thursday last a publican in Shoreditch sold his wife for a ticket in the present lottery, on condition that if the ticket be drawn blank, he is to have his wife again as soon as the drawing of the lottery is over.'

Lost and found

Wives were also sold through small ads in newspapers, usually headlined A BARGAIN TO BE SOLD. One farmer advertised for the return of a horse he had lost through a London paper. He offered five guineas (£5.25) for it. The following day, his wife ran away. He offered four shillings (20p) for her recovery.

Beer money

A Westminster donkey driver sold his wife and his donkey to another donkey driver for 13 shillings (65p) and two pots of beer. This being England, the two men and the newly sold wife repaired to the pub to drink the beer. On 30 January 1817, another wife vendor, a man of means, stood the man who purchased his wife a pint of beer to drink his health in. The woman had fetched just 1s 6d – 7½p – but the vendor was delighted to be rid of her.

On 9 December 1819, a man sold his wife to a painter for 5s 6d – 27½p. An itinerant carpenter was even more put out when he sold his wife to a mate, only to discover that she had unexpectedly inherited £1,500 a few weeks later.

Rope trick

A labourer in Oxford pocketed the princely sum of £5 for his wife. He held onto the rope until he got the money, then wished the purchaser the best of luck. But an Essex man got only half a crown (12½p) for his wife and two children. The wife was led around the village of Marchin Green with a rope around her neck to the accompaniment of music.

These formalities were plainly important. A man in Thame, Oxfordshire, sold his wife without leading her about on a rope. Later he was told that the sale was not valid, so he took his wife back, led her on a seven-mile trek around Thame and sold her for half a crown. He was then liable for fourpence (2p) tax, the same amount as was levied on the sale of livestock.

And it was not just husbands who could sell wives. In February 1790, a man in Swadlincote, Derbyshire, absconded, leaving his wife on the parish. The head of the parish council took her to nearby Burton-on-Trent, where he sold her for a florin (10p). The sale appeared in the parish accounts, which note that the price of the rope was included.

Wife selling continued into Victorian times and the prices had not got any better. At the sale attended by hundreds of people in Dudley in 1859 the highest bid was still sixpence. Three years later, at Selby, Yorkshire, the highest bid was a pint of beer. Though in 1881, in Sheffield the price seems to have gone up to a quart. But at Alfreton, a man again accepted a pint of beer, just to get rid of his wife, while in Ireland, according to the *Pall Mall Gazette* of 20 October 1882, George Drennan sold his wife to Patrick O'Neill for one penny and a dinner.

Husband for sale

The sale of husbands occurred less frequently. However, in Drogheda, one Margaret Collins complained to the local magistrate that her husband was living with another woman as man and wife. The husband told the court that his wife was a harridan who frequently bit him in rage. His new wife had offered tuppence for him, but had eventually purchased him for just 1½d. It seems that husbands fetched even less than wives. The court found the transaction perfectly legal and the plaintiff did nothing to help her case by leaping at the newly-weds in a frenzy, having to be dragged off.

A harem near Heathrow

As a young man, Lord Baltimore had given up his position at court and had headed for the Orient, where he indulged his love of women. When he returned to Britain, he built a large house on the western outskirts of London, which he organised like the harem in Constantinople, though stocked with local women. Every material whim of the beautiful girls he collected there was catered for. However, they were not allowed out and the strict rules of the harem were policed by older women.

In 1808, one of the inmates, a milliner by the name of Sarah Woodcock, escaped and accused Baltimore of rape. However, the jury at Kingston assizes found that the women in his seraglio had not been coerced into sex. They were there willingly and Baltimore was acquitted.

Afterwards, he left England and travelled around Europe with a harem of eight and two black *corregidores* to police them. When he arrived in Vienna, Count von Schrotten-bach asked him which of the eight was his wife. Baltimore replied that he did not care to stay in a country where he could be asked such an impertinent question, nor one where the matter could not be settled with a duel, so he immediately left Austria.

Divorce by horse, of course

The gypsies who inhabited old England could rid themselves an unwanted spouses by the use of a horse. The animal was to be in perfect health and as free from defects as possible. In the morning, it was let loose and its movements observed. Its behaviour was supposed to indicate the extent of the woman's guilt – only the woman, it seems, could be at fault in the break-down of a marriage. A master of ceremonies was then picked by lot. He then charged the horse with the woman's alleged crimes. Then, as near to midday as possible, he took a knife and plunged it into the heart of the animal.

When the horse was dead, its carcass was stretched out on the ground. The man and woman then held hands over the dead animal and intoned the words of the Romany divorce. Afterwards they let go and circled the corpse, repeating the words. Finally, they shook hands and parted.

The woman was then given a piece of cast iron with the letter T on it. Meanwhile the horse's heart was cut out and roasted on a fire, then sprinkled with brandy or vinegar and eaten by the divorced husband and his friends. The rest of the carcass was buried. In the subsequent years, they would return to the grave to see that it had not been disturbed and to mourn the dead marriage.

Incest

In his book *Sexual Life in England*, the German sexologist Ivan Bloch mentions that incest was common in England, due to the appalling slums where father and daughter, mother and son, brother and sister all had to sleep together in the same bed. However, the two examples of incest he cites come from north of the border.

The first is the case of Major Thomas Weir. Born in Lanark in 1600, he served as a lieutenant in the Scottish Puritan – Covenanter – army in the English Civil War. After the war he became a civil servant and an admired religious fanatic. Suddenly, at the age of 70, he began confessing a lifetime of terrible sins. At first no one believed him and, when he persisted, the provost, or chief magistrate, sent for a doctor. But Weir was found to be sane and 'his distemper only an exulcerated conscience', so the provost was forced to arrest him.

Weir came to trial on 9 April 1670, indicted on four counts involving the attempted rape of his sister, Jane, when she was 10, and continued incest with her from when she was 16 to 50; incest with his stepdaughter, Margaret Bourdon, the daughter of his deceased wife; several counts of adultery; and bestiality with mares and cows.

The Weirs' sister-in-law Margaret testified that, at the age of 27, she found the major, her brother-in-law and her sister-in-law lying naked together in a barn. There was also a witness to the major's bestiality with a mare. A woman had seen him in the act and complained. But no one had believed her and she was 'whipped through the town by the hands of the common hangman, [for] slander of such an eminent holy man'.

Weir's sister Jane was also charged with incest and 'most especially consulting witches, necromancers and devils'.

The jury found Jane Weir guilty on a unanimous vote. Major Thomas Weir was convicted by a majority verdict. He was strangled and burned on the execution ground between Leith and 60-year-old Jane was burned the following day at the Grass Market in Edinburgh.

The second case is that of Sawney Beane from East Lothian, who lived in the reign of James I of Scotland (1406–37). He eloped with a young woman 'equally idle and profligate' and they went to live in a cave in a remote part of Galloway. From there, they robbed and murdered passers-by, and survived by eating the bodies of their victims. They had six daughters and eight sons. Incest then provided them with 14 granddaughters and 18 grandsons.

Their 25-year crime spree was brought to an end when a man escaped after seeing his wife murdered. The King himself with 400 followers went to track the Beane clan down. They entered Beane's cave and men found a treasure trove of stolen goods on the floor, and the pieces of the corpses of men, women and children hung from the ceiling like chunks of cured meat. The family – now numbering 21 females and 27 males – were taken to Edinburgh, where they were put to death without trial. The men had their hands and feet cut off and their intestines torn out and were left to bleed to death. After being forced to watch this, the women were burned to death on three separate fires. It was noted that all died without the least sign of repentance and continued shouting filthy curses to the last.

CHAPTER SIX

Prostitution

OVE ASIDE, PARIS, Amsterdam, Venice, Hamburg: *London* was Europe's capital of prostitution. In 1853, the British medical journal the *Lancet* reported that in 'no Continental capital is it possible to see society so shockingly in the grip of vice and debauchery as in our own metropolis'.

Oldest profession

Things were much the same in 1729, according to the book *Satan's Harvest Home, or the Present State of Fornication, Adultery, Whorecraft, Procuring, Pimping, Sodomy and the Game at Flatts* – this last was lesbianism, which was thought to involve a certain amount of flattery. The author observed,

> When a person unacquainted with the town, passes at night through any of our principal streets, he is apt to wonder whence that vast body of courtezans, which stand ready, on

small purchase to obey the laws of nature and gratify the lust of every drunken Rake-hell, can take its rise.

At one time it was estimated that possibly as many as one woman in eight in London was on the game.

Shamelessness

Foreign observers were particularly critical. Hector France commented on the coarseness and shamelessness of prostitution in England. The Russian anthropologist Professor Benjamin Tarnowsky said that prostitution was not practised in so cynical a fashion in any other European city. And the author of *On the History, Statistics and Regulation of Prostitution*, published in Austria in 1865, said that in no other country was prostitution so widespread and carried on in such a shameless and bestial fashion. This may have been because the thriving trade in London attracted prostitutes from all over the

Continent. Without the prostitutes, it was noted, 'many thousand houses would stand empty'.

Marylebone

In the late eighteenth century it was estimated that there were at least 13,000 prostitutes in the fashionable newly built-up parish of Marylebone alone, of whom 1,700 inhabited whole houses.

'These last live very respectably and are undisturbed in the exercise of their profession,' said a foreign visitor, adding that they often lived in charming, well-furnished houses, with maids, and some even received annuities 'from their seducers or from rich and generous lovers when intoxicated. These annuities certainly secure them from need, but they are usually not sufficient to enable them to live sumptuously in the capital and to enjoy expensive pleasures; they therefore permit lovers' visits, but only those who they like – the others are sent away.'

Lower-class prostitutes could not be so picky. They lived together in open houses, under the supervision of matrons who provided them with food and clothing. Even lower-class girls were supplied with silk gowns, though. Some were tempted to flee with their finery and set up on their own account. This meant a girl could pick and choose her client, which was not allowed in the managed houses. The disadvantage was that she had to provide for herself and many freelance prostitutes ended up in debtors' prisons.

The price of prostitution

The author James Boswell (1740–95) enjoyed 'free-hearted ladies of all kinds: from the splendid Madam at fifty guineas a night' – £52.50 or £6,000 in today's money – 'down to the civil nymph with white-thread stockings who tramps down the Strand and will resign her engaging person to your honour for a pint of wine and a shilling' – 5p or less than £6 at today's prices. It took an ordinary working man three hours to earn a shilling, and it was enough to pay the rent of a cheap lodging in a garret or basement for a week.

The satirist John Wolcott (1738–1819), who wrote under the name Peter Pindar, obviously went with a better class of hooker. He attended gatherings where 'every woman is accomplished, every woman is handsome … and more than a half of those Cleopatras are to be purchased for half-a-crown'.

With cheap whores there were hidden costs. One woman with whom Boswell enjoyed a brief coupling in Whitehall Gardens used the opportunity to steal a handkerchief from his pocket, leaving him 'shocked to think that I had been intimately united with a low, abandoned, perjured, pilfering creature'. On the other hand there were pleasures to be had for free. One day in Covent Garden, Boswell 'met two very pretty little girls who asked me to take them with me'. He explained that he had no money to pay them. Nevertheless they went with him to a private room in the Shakespeare Head, where he had sex with both of them.

But Boswell's greatest thrill seems to come from the location of his encounters. One day he met 'a strong, jolly young damsel' outside St James's Palace and had her on Westminster Bridge. 'The whim of doing it there with the Thames rolling below us amused me every much,' he wrote. A few weeks later he picked up 'a fresh, agreeable young girl called Alice Gibbs' in Downing Street.

Harris's List

It was not necessary to pick girls up on the street. A selection appeared in *Harris's List of Covent-Garden Ladies*, which appeared annually from 1760 to 1793 and sold around 8,000 copies a time. Harris had been head waiter at the Shakespeare Tavern and began simply publishing the details of the women who plied their trade there. Later, he cast his net more widely and promised that, by his researches, 'we shall be able to suit every constitution, and every pocket, every whim and fancy that the most extravagant sensualist can desire ...'

About 80 women appeared in each edition and the listings gave their name, address, physical attributes, specialities and charges. Here are a couple of examples:

Miss Burn, No. 18, Old Compton Street, Soho

Close in the arms she languishingly lies,
With dying looks, short breath, and wishing eyes.

This accomplished nymph has just attained her eighteenth year, and fraught with every perfection, enters a volunteer in the field of Venus. She plays on the piano forte, sings, dances, and is mistress of every Manoeuvre in the amorous contest that can enhance the coming pleasure ... her price is two pounds two.

Miss Johnson, No. 17, Goodge Street, Charlotte Street.

And all these joys insatiably to prove,
With which rich beauty feasts the glutton love.

The raven coloured tresses of Miss Johnson are pleasing, and are characteristics of strength and ability in the wars of Venus … She has such a noble elasticity in her loins, that she can cast her lover to a pleasing height, and receive him again with the utmost dexterity. Her price is one pound one …

On average, a whole night with one of these women cost two guineas, roughly what an ordinary working man earned in two weeks. It is estimated that full-time prostitution alone turned over more than £10 million a year in the last decades of the eighteenth century, while the London building trade in the same period was worth less than half that.

After *Harris's List* had folded, the *Ranger's Magazine* ran a 'monthly list of the Covent Garden Cyprians; or the man of pleasure's *vade mecum*' (handy or useful book) in 1795. And from 1842 to 1844 the short-lived publication the *Exquisite* ran much the same service under headings such as STARS OF THE SALONS, SEDUCTION UNVEILED and SKETCHES OF COURTESANS.

Police protection

The reason why prostitutes could operate so openly was that they were protected by the law. The nineteenth-century German pornographic novel *Memoirs of a Singer* – translated into English as *Promiscuous Pauline* – mentioned that, in London, 'The street girls, although they are called prostitutes in the police reports, are at the same time not such social pariahs as on the Continent, and they are better protected by law than elsewhere; if they are insulted by anyone, or called dishonourable names, the offender is punished; they are also not so shunned as a class as in other places, and for this reason they do not call themselves prostitutes, but independent ladies.'

The Habeas Corpus Act of 1679 also protected brothel owners. It meant that constables did not dare enter a building unless a crime was actually being committed or they had a magistrate's warrant. To make a complaint, two taxpayers from the same parish had to appear before a JP and pay £50 for the collection of evidence and £20 against the costs of the prosecution. Only then would an arrest warrant be issued.

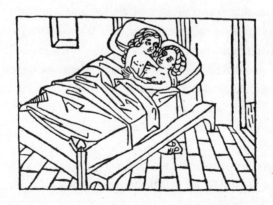

To secure a conviction, a witness would have to admit in open court that the accused had committed an act of immorality in the establishment in question. If a defendant feared this might happen, she could simply move to another parish where the proceedings would have to begin all over again.

When the Metropolitan Police were established in London in 1829, they quickly found themselves the ally of the prostitutes, who paid the police an average of £3 a week to keep their eyes closed. This was in the bobbies' interest too. Most were bachelors and lived in barracks. They needed the service the prostitutes provided.

Doings in London

In his book *Doings in London; or Day and Night Scenes of the Frauds, Frolics, Manners, and Depravities of the Metropolis*, published in 1828, George Smeeton divided the capital's prostitutes into four distinct types. There were 'hackneyed' prostitutes who went about their business for small sums in dark alleys by 'forcing men into their disgusting embraces by every art and trick that wantonness and wickedness can invent'. They usually had venereal disease and were often accompanied by a thug who would rob the client.

There were girls who worked in a 'house of retreat'. They paid over almost all their fees to the madam, in exchange for food, clothing and a roof over their head. There was a lot of theft and robbery in these 'schools of debauchery', as Smeeton called them.

There were the higher-class girls who worked in the 'private bagnios [brothels] of the West End'. They had procuresses, 'flash-men', landlords and servants, all of whom 'make a considerable living out of them'.

And there were 'the prostitutes of fashion, the refuse and cast-off mistresses of men of quality who reserve themselves only for such as are able, by ample fortunes, to pay for the favours they bestow …'

The first edition of *Doings in London*, which renders all this useful information, is dedicated to Robert Peel, the home secretary who set up the Metropolitan Police the following year.

Prostitution in London

Published in 1839, *Prostitution in London* was a serious work, written by Michael Ryan for the Society for the Suppression of Vice. In it he added two more classes of prostitute. One class comprised soldiers' prostitutes, canteen women and sailors' prostitutes, who worked along the Thames. These came from the lowest levels of society.

Then there were the ordinary working girls who prostituted themselves for extra cash. According to Ryan, they included milliners, bonnet makers, furriers, shoe binders, shop workers and frequenters of theatres, fairs and dancing rooms.

'It is impossible to estimate the number of those addicted to secret prostitution in the different ranks of society,' Ryan concluded.

On top of this, Georgiana Hill, author of *Women in English Life: From Medieval to Modern Times*, published in 1896, said that most married men in England kept mistresses and 'Some have carried them home and made them eat at the same table with their wives, and yet no mischief has happened …' the only distinction being that 'they are handsomer for the most part, better dressed and less starch'd'.

The ages of prostitutes

James Beard Talbot carried out a survey of 3,103 prostitutes in 1838. Of them, three were under 15; 414 were between 14 and 20; 872 were between 20 and 25; 525 were between 25 and 30; 237 were between 30 and 40; 88 were between 40 and 50; and 29 were between 50 and 60 – though most over 50 had moved on to become procuresses or brothel keepers.

There were an estimated 5,000 procurers and procuresses in London in 1850 and Ryan calculated that there were more than 400,000 people directly or indirectly involved in the sex trade.

According to the author of *The Great Metropolis*, published in 1836, 'not one young man in one hundred can be met who has not had connexion with lewd women'.

Mother Needham

The madam Elizabeth Needham was so notorious that she appeared in William Hogarth's series of engravings *A Harlot's Progress* of *c.* 1731, procuring 'strong, lusty, and country wenches with buttocks as hard as Cedar Cheeses' for the notorious debauchee, the wealthy Scot, Colonel Francis Charteris. Throughout the 1720s, her name appeared regularly in the papers, which noted that she also worked under the names Mother Bird, Blewit and Howard.

When her brothel in Conduit Street near Hanover Square burned down, killing a French army officer, she moved to

Union Street near Bond Street. Eventually she was convicted for running a disorderly house in Park Place, St James's. She was fined one shilling and sentenced to stand in the pillory. On 30 April 1731, the sentence was carried out and she was so severely pelted that she died from her injuries a few days later.

Panders

While women became bawds (a term applied to women in the eighteenth century who ran brothels) men became panders. According to Richard King's *The Frauds of London Detected*, they were usually French – cooks, barmen and valets who masqueraded as gentlemen and made out that they knew the 'most accomplished belles in Paris, with whom they were on the very best of terms'. Noblemen would employ them to tour the Continent to bring back willing partners. King said, sniffily, that no Englishman could play the role so well.

Trappers

'Big-bellied' harlots would work with 'trappers' in a simple blackmail scam. When they spotted a mark alone in a public place, the rotund prostitute and one of the trappers would approach him. According to King's *The Frauds of London Detected*, the harlot would then say to her companion, 'Jack, that is the gentleman that did so and so with me at such and such a time.'

'Is it?' said her associate. 'I know him well, and so shall the world too, I'll blow him to the Devil.'

Another associate approached and whispered in the mark's ear, proposing that he give hush money to the other two, 'who are capable to committing any wickedness'. If he refused, they started an argument. A crowd would gather. A fight would break out and the mark would often get the worst of it. If the mark handed over cash, the trappers would find out where he lived and continue the blackmail.

Naturally, any man who visited a brothel was also vulnerable, especially if he carried papers giving his address. He could easily find himself paying for the upkeep of a prostitute and her illegitimate offspring.

Bullies

A 'bully' was a prostitute's protector, though he would often work for more than one woman. Sometimes they would subsidise their income from the girls by robbing – even murdering – their client. The Fleet Ditch area of Farringdon was known as the 'bullies quarter'.

There 'almost every house is the lowest and most infamous brothel', according to a doctor who attended the girls. The Ditch itself was a large open sewer where the bullies would toss the bodies of their victims, which would then be washed into the Thames.

Extortion

The German sexologist Ivan Bloch reported the case of two young men who were picked up by two 'apparently virtuous women, about twenty years of age' in a carriage in one of the royal parks and whisked home to 'a most notoriously infamous square in the metropolis', where 'all was folly and debauchery until the next morning'.

They were just about to leave when they were told they must pay more money. When they said they had no more, but would call again, 'their vicious companions yelled vociferously. Two desperate-looking villains, accompanied by a large mastiff, now entered the apartment, and threatened to murder the delinquents if they did not immediately pay more money.

A frightful fight ensued; the mastiff seized one of the assaulted by the thigh [and] tore out a considerable portion of flesh.'

Summoned by the commotion, a large crowd assembled and attacked the house, nearly demolishing it, while the two young men made good their escape. They were lucky. When a brothel was demolished in a nearby court, several skeletons were found under the floor.

Country coaches

The demand for women in Georgian times was so high that madams were always on the lookout for new girls. According to a German visitor in the eighteenth century, 'These vile procuresses like to keep their eye on the country coaches which arrive daily in London in great numbers from the provinces, and usually bring in country girls seeking service in the capital.'

Georgiana Hill, author of *Women in English Life*, agreed: 'One of the causes of the number of these *filles de joie* was, probably, the constant immigration from the provinces of young friendless girls eager to taste the delights of London. When their means were exhausted it was impossible for them to obtain employment without credentials, and they entered upon the only career that seemed open to them.'

Even the daughters of country parsons fell into prostitution this way.

In *The Frauds of London Detected*, Richard King said that there would be a crowd of bawds hanging around the terminuses, or even the previous stopping places, 'to pick countrymen for old stales' – unchaste women – 'or countrywomen for old lechers'.

Like mother, like daughter

Some girls were simply bred for prostitution. In *Prostitution in London*, Michael Ryan recorded the case of Leah Davis, who brought up all 13 of her daughters to be prostitutes and kept brothels with them all over town. Mothers often sold their daughters into prostitution. Charles II's mistress Nell Gwyn started her working life as a prostitute in Mrs Ross's bawdy house in Drury Lane, where her mother sold ale. Her price was half a crown – 12½p or £13 at today's prices. The Earl of Rochester recruited her, trying her out before putting her in the way of the King.

According to Ryan, one in every three of the daughters of 'persons in the lower rank' became a prostitute before the age of 20.

Fresh blood

Another source of fresh blood was the factories. It has been estimated that in 1793, of the 50,000 prostitutes in London, some 20 were factory workers, while only 3,000 came from domestic service. However, the barmaids and waitresses in the inns in the nineteenth century often entered into casual prostitution with the guests.

Shopkeepers hung notices in their windows announcing vacancies for working girls, then introduced the applicants to prostitution. Some kept a clandestine brothel above or at the back of the shop. And fortune tellers and the sellers of erotic books would often act as talent scouts.

Then there were also homeless street girls who had little choice but to sell themselves.

'What a pitiful sight it is to see a crowd of little creatures lying in heaps close to one another,' said the book *Satan's Harvest Home*, 'how even in the severest weather they sleep in the streets, and how some of them, hardly big enough to reach a man's hip, are already pregnant and a burden on the parish whose dung-heap serves them as a refuge!'

Foreign imports

Panders from London would travel on the Continent procuring young women ostensibly as governesses, dressmakers and domestic servants, pay their first quarter's salary, then sell them at a high price to a London brothel. And German, Belgian, Italian and Greek prostitutes had drifted to London because of its wealth and reputation, along with the French, who had fled there to escape the Revolution. Londoners called all foreign prostitutes 'French women' and they enjoyed a reputation for bringing a special refinement to all the arts of love.

Then there were girls from the East and West Indies. The English had developed a taste for black prostitutes early on.

Places of business

Along with theatres, churches were a major centre of prostitution. They had been fashionable places for the young to gather since the sixteenth century. The youth of London would gather outside St Paul's Cathedral to laugh, gossip and parade their new clothes. This was such a well-established practice that young bucks paid compensation to the church authorities for the noise their spurs made.

In *Prostitution in London*, Michael Ryan noted that not only would girls wait for men coming out of church to accost them, men would proposition women at the door of the church and take them to one of the brothels that had sprung up in the vicinity.

Brothels also sprang up around the Law Courts and the Houses of Parliament, where they would be certain of a stiff trade. St Bartholomew's Hospital allowed prostitutes to use their cloisters to ply their trade, according to the *Observer* of 21 August 1703. Being 'in the cloisters' developed a meaning of its own. Meanwhile, high-class prostitutes could be seen in the royal parks, parading around in open coaches pulled by elegant ponies.

For lower-class prostitutes there was the Port of London. Girls would often travel from London to other ports when the arrival of a ship was announced. The ensuing orgies helped fuel the spread of venereal disease.

Window shopping

Just as in Amsterdam today, in old England prostitutes displayed themselves in windows. Consequently, respectable woman avoided windows at all costs.

'To show oneself is considered very improper,' wrote a German visitor in the eighteenth century. 'Nothing less than an unusual incident in the street could excuse an honourable woman opening the window. Public girls, on the other hand, interpret this morality the other way round.'

In the 1830s, girls stood naked in the windows of the notorious Aubrey brothel. They often adopted all sorts of indecent poses and performed lewd actions. These performances were soon emulated by rival houses and visitors to Victorian London were shocked to see young ladies at what they took to be a girls' school displaying themselves naked in the windows and making lubricious gestures.

The manhunt

In the late eighteenth century, the German writer J.W. von Archenoltz observed a nightly ritual. He wrote,

> As soon as it gets dark, these girls, well turned out, in all seasons flood the principal streets and squares of the town. Many go on the manhunt in borrowed clothes which they hire by the day from the madams, who for safety's sake pay

another woman to follow the huntress on foot to see that the other girl does not run away with the clothes.

If a girl came home without money, he wrote, she would be 'ill-treated and must go hungry', so they would accost passers-by and take them home or to a tavern. He goes on,

Many married women too, who live in distant parts of the city, come to Westminster where they are not known and carry on their profession, either from vice or need. I have been astounded to see children of eight and nine years offer their company, at least as far as it would serve.

In *Letters from London*, F. W. von Schütz described a similar scene:

It is certain that no place in the world can be compared to London for wantonness ... What struck me most was the shamelessness of the children who, with the grownups, roamed the streets and offered their services to passers-by.

Haymarket

Prostitution and other night life depended on street lighting. In the eighteenth century, it was observed that London had more oil lamps lighting the streets than any other town in Europe. Then came gas lighting, which was first installed in Finsbury Square in 1808. It quickly spread to the West End and the centre of prostitution moved from the narrow lanes of

Drury Lane and Covent Garden to the broad thoroughfares of Haymarket and Regent Street.

In 1862, Julius Rodenberg wrote,

> While sleep rules in London's huge circumference and even the dance halls are dark and still, the 'Café de la Régence' is still lighted up, and on the wide pavement as far as the columns of His Majesty's Theatre begins the promenade which seldom ends before two or three in the morning.

CHAPTER SEVEN

Brothels and Stews

OMAN-STYLE PUBLIC baths were reintroduced to Europe by the returning Crusaders, who had enjoyed warm baths in the Middle East. In England they rapidly degenerated into brothels. During the reign of Henry II (1154–89), bathhouse brothels were set up on the south bank of the Thames in Southwark. This area lay outside the city walls and did not become part of the capital until 1550. They were called *bagnios* – from *bagno*, the Italian word for bath – or 'stewhouses', as clients of the baths 'stewed' in the hot water there.

House rules

In his *Survey of London* of 1633, John Stow noted that the bordellos and stews of the Borough of Southwark were regulated by a law passed in 1161, among whose rules were that 'no stew-holder, or his wife, should let or stay any single woman to go and come freely at all times, when they listed'. Further, 'No stew-holder [was] to keep any woman to boord, but she to boord abroad at her pleasure', and he was to 'take no more for the woman's chamber in the week, than fourteen pence'.

There were other rules: he should not keep his doors open or keep a single woman in his house on holy days; no single woman was to be kept against her will; no stew-holder was to receive any woman of religion, or any man's wife.

A single woman was not to take money to 'lie with any man, except she lie with him all night until the morrow'; and a stew-holder was not 'to keep any woman that hath the perilous infirmity of burning' and was 'not to sell bread, ale, flesh, fish, wood, coal or any victuals etc.'.

This law was reconfirmed by Edward III and Henry IV. And, in a new city law of 1351, girls working in the bagnios were banned from wearing certain items of clothing usually worn by the nobility.

The Cardinal's Hat

In the twelfth century there were 18 bagnios in Southwark. As few people could read, they were identified, like pubs, by a sign outside. These included the Castle, the Crane, the Bell, the Boar's Head and the Cardinal's Hat. This last was appropriate, as the house was supervised by the Bishop of Winchester.

In 1380, the bagnios of Southwark belonged to a fish-monger named William Walworth, who was also lord mayor of London. But he left day-to-day management to a madam.

The pious and studious Henry VI (1422–61 and 1470–1) closed the bagnios down, but the demand was so great he was forced to open them again. However, their number was limited to 12. In 1546, towards the end of his reign, Henry VIII finally closed them. According to John Stow, he sent a herald into the streets of Southwark to blow a trumpet and invite the women working there to 'keep good and honest rule'. He did not say whether this was successful. It may simply have spread the problem.

Private brothels

The aristocratic mansions of the Elizabethan era were so large that they often had a brothel operating inside them. There was one run by a Mrs Higgens in the London establishment of the Earl of Worcester. When the constables closed it, the earl, far from being grateful, sued the officers at the King's Bench.

In the mid-1570s, a Holborn brothel keeper named John Hollingbrig wore the livery of Lord Ambrose Dudley, Earl of Warwick. His brother Lord Robert Dudley and other privy councillors intervened to oppose indictments when the authorities attempted to crack down on prostitution.

It's thought that a male brothel in Hoxton was owned by Lord Hunsdon. And there are references to a male stew at Aldersgate – Cock Lane – called Madame Caesar's, where aristocratic women would repair to eat 'apricocks ungelt'.

Cleanliness is next to godliness

By the beginning of the seventeenth century, there were prostitutes all over London and the city's aldermen made an attempt to arrest girls who solicited in taverns. They fined the owners of the bagnios that had now spread way beyond Southwark £20 if they allowed girls to work there, or allowed young men and other reprobates into baths normally reserved for women. The Puritans enforced these laws rigorously. But even under the Commonwealth there was a need to keep clean. In 1649 Peter Chamberlen, a physician, petitioned Parliament to establish baths right across England. His petition was turned down on the grounds that baths would be a threat to public morality.

Ladies' nights

With the Restoration, bathhouses reverted to their former use as brothels. In the eighteenth century Covent Garden became the centre of the bagnio business. The most fashionable bagnio there belonged a Molly King, and it heaved with libertines and prostitutes of all ranks. She earned a fortune and retired. Mother Douglas – also known as Mother Cole – ran an establishment that catered only for the crème de la crème. It was said that princes and peers frequented it, along with women of rank who visited incognito.

Aristocratic ladies also visited Mrs Gould's in Covent Garden, though anyone who carried on an indecent conversation or swore was thrown out. The men who visited were usually rich merchants who pretended that they were spending the weekend in the country but actually turned up at Mrs Gould's bagnio on a Saturday evening and stayed until Monday morning. They were provided with 'the most excellent liquors, very refined courtesans, the most elegant beds and furniture'. She steered clear of the law because her lover was a public notary.

A visitor's view

The German traveller Archenholtz visited a London bathhouse in the late eighteenth century.

'In London there are certain kinds of houses, called bagnios,' he wrote. These posed as baths, but their real purpose was 'to provide persons of both sexes with pleasure'. The houses contained 'every device for exciting the senses'. Girls were fetched in chairs when needed.

Only women who were particularly attractive were sent for, so girls would circulate their names and addresses to hundreds of bagnios in the hope of making themselves known. A girl who was sent for and did not please did not get paid, though the customer had to pay for the chair anyway.

Archenholtz was amazed at how seriously the English took the whole business: 'The English retain their solemnity even in their pleasures, and consequently the business of such a house is conducted with a seriousness and propriety that is hard to credit.'

Court houses

After the Hanoverian succession, the gulf between the aristocracy and ordinary people widened. Courtiers no longer frequented common brothels and bagnios, but maintained
houses of their own. A German observer noted, 'There are
houses in the vicinity of St James's Palace where nymphs are
kept for the pleasure of the courtiers.'

They lived under well-to-do matrons, he observed, paid for
their apartments and food and were treated as boarders, but
had to submit to the rules of the house.

'The high price paid even for entry to these temples kept
the mob from entering,' he wrote. 'This attracted the wealthy
and distinguished all the more. The famous [Charles James]
Fox, before he became a minister [he was Britain's first foreign
secretary in 1782] was one of the many visitors to these houses,
and often hurried straight from there to Parliament ...'

Fox eventually domesticated his vices: he married a courtesan, Elizabeth Bridget, former mistress of the Prince of Wales.

Mrs Goadby's seraglios

In 1750, a seraglio was opened in Berwick Street, Soho, by Mrs
Goadby after she had been to Paris to see how such premises
there were run. Like the Parisian houses, she tried to provide
only the most beautiful girls and a wide variety of women from
different countries and backgrounds. Doctors gave them regular check-ups and she dressed them in fine laces and silks.

Mrs Goadby was a strict taskmistress and the girls were
duty-bound to show the utmost zeal and sincerity when 'per-

forming the rites and ceremonies of the Cyprian goddess'. In contrast to those in the French *sérails*, the girl were allowed to drink – though they were neither to drink nor eat too much. But the most unpardonable sin was to hide gifts they received from clients on top of the fee paid to the brothel.

From midday until the evening the girls spent their time in a large salon singing and embroidering. Clients usually arrived after the theatre. One might offer the girl of his choice a handkerchief. If she accepted, she was his for the night. In France, the girl and a good dinner cost just one *louis d'or* – about £1 – though the price in England was considerably higher.

Mrs Goadby's aim, she said, was to 'refine the Englishman's amorous amusement' and her girls were to indulge their clients' fantasies, whims and requirements in every detail, though in all other ways they were to be modest and demur. Once her clientele discovered that they were allowed to indulge any fantasy or perversion they wished – and as she did not charge the low prices of French brothels – Mrs Goadby became very rich and, eventually, retired to the country. Others quickly followed her example and opened luxurious brothels – though none so extravagant as a brothel in Amsterdam, called the Fountain, that boasted a restaurant, a café, a dancehall and a rooftop billiards room where the most beautiful girls played billiards naked while gentlemen looked on.

The Cloister

Soon after Mrs Goadby set up shop, a notorious courtesan named Charlotte Hayes opened her 'Cloister' in King's Place, Pall Mall. The beautiful 'nuns' there were hand-picked – 'select

merchandise', as Charlotte called them – and trained personally by Hayes, who was vastly experienced after numerous
amorous adventures of her own. The girls were supplied with
expensive jewellery and adornments as well as food and clothing. Everything was charged to their account. Soon they were
so deeply in debt that they could not leave.

*Nocturnal Revels: or, the History of King's-Place and other
Modern Nunneries* (1779) reproduced the supposed records of
Charlotte Hayes's Cloister for Sunday, 9 January. As the book
was printed at the behest of Mrs Goadby, and certainly produced with Mrs Goadby's help, it may be a spoof, but it
undoubtedly provided insider information. It volunteered, 'To
see Charlotte's bill of fare, upon these occasions, would make
a cynic smile.'

First on the menu was: 'A maid for Alderman Drybones –
Nell Blossom, about nineteen, has not been in company for
four days and was prepared for a state of vestalship last night.'
The price was 20 guineas – £21, or £2,400 at today's prices.

Others included a 'bona roba for Lord Spasm'; 'Sir Harry
Flagellum, exactly at nine; Nell Hardy from Bow-Street, or Bet
Flourish from Berners-Street, or Mrs Birch herself from
Chapel-Street ...'

Charlotte also provided men for women, for a fee. The bill
of fare went on:

Lady Loveit, just come from Bath, much disappointed in her
amour with Lord Atall; desires to go upon sure ground, and
be well mounted this evening, before she goes to the
Duchess of Basto's route. – Captain O'Thunder, or Sawney
Rawbone. Fifty guineas.

Then there were men who craved more seemingly innocent pleasures: 'His Excellency Count Alto – a woman of fashion, for *la bagatelle* only, for about an hour. Mrs O'Smirk, just come from Dunkirk, or Miss Graceful, from Paddington. Ten guineas.' Accordingly:

The Doctor was mounted in the three-pair-of-stairs; Lady Loveit had the drawing room, the sofa, and the adjoining tent-bed; Alderman Drybones was crammed in the chintz bed-chamber, which, though small, is elegant, and used only upon vestal occasions; Sir Harry Flagellum was whipped in the nursery, where there were accommodations for every sort to please him; Lord Spasm had the high French bed-room; the Colonel took his chance in the parlour upon the settee; and the Count and Lord Pyebald were entertained in the saloon of chastity and the Card-Room.

If the figures are to be believed, Charlotte Hayes made over £135 – or £15,000 today – for that single day's work. She retired with £20,000 – over £1.5 million today – and set up as a country lady.

West End girls

Other seraglios sprang up in King's Place. One was run by a black woman named Miss Harriot, who also had a number of distinguished lovers. She had been brought over from Jamaica by her master, who had been struck down by smallpox and died, leaving Miss Harriot free to embark on her new career. Mrs Prendergast ran another place, while Mrs Mitchell's famously carried the inscription *in medio tutissimus* – 'safety is in the middle course'.

Susannah Adams opened a brothel in Westminster. Former prostitute Lucy Cooper ran one in Bond Street, while a woman named Hannah ran a number of them in Johnson's Court. And there was one in Holborn that offered a luncheon service at midday.

Mrs Nelson, a faded beauty, set up shop at the corner of Holland and Wardour Streets in Soho. To provide her clients with fresh 'wares', she took a job as a governess in a school to entice young girls into the profession. As soon as a new girl was on the books, her 'husband' Mr Nelson sent a circular to all their wealthy clients.

Black beauties

Black women were very much in demand in England in the eighteenth century. The Duke of Clarence, later William IV, brought a Jamaican beauty called 'Wowski' back from the West Indies with him and a black woman named Harriet – probably the brothel keeper Miss Harriot – appeared in Hogarth's etching *The Discovery*.

English women, it seems, preferred Arab men. Beturbaned

Arabs were seen hanging about on street corners where ladies' maids would approach them to arrange assignations with their mistresses. Usually, it was said, these were women who were 'supported or neglected by rich men, and naturally of easy virtue'.

London pederasts also had a penchant for Arab boys.

Translation service

In the early nineteenth century Mary Wilson ran a series of lavish brothels in Tonbridge Place, Old Bond Street, New Road, St Pancras and Hall Place, St John's Wood. She also translated erotic books, including *The Voluptuous Night, The Whore's Catechism*, Aretino's *The Accomplished Whore* and Mirabeau's *The Education of Laura*. In addition, she published four volumes of *The Voluptuarian Cabinet* under the epigraph '*Dum futuimus vivimus*' – 'while we fuck we live'.

Equal rights

There were brothels in the eighteenth century that catered to women, too. Mrs Redon's in Bolton Street, Piccadilly, did not employ regular prostitutes. Rather, she used ladies of a better class who wanted to amuse themselves with young male clients. In Curzon Street, Mayfair, Mrs Banks also provided 'vigorous men' for ladies of breeding. But she also laid on voluptuous young women in the hope that the men would become her clients too.

Mary Wilson proposed going further. In *The Voluptuarian Cabinet* she outlined her plan for an

Eleusinian Institute, to which any lady of rank and means may subscribe to this Institute, and to which she may repair incognito; the married to commit what the world calls adultery, the single to commit what at the Tabernacle is termed fornication, or in gentler phrase, to obey the dictates of all-powerful nature, by offering up a cheerful sacrifice to the god Priapus ...

In this 'most elegant temple' with its 'large saloons', men amused themselves and the ladies were able to view them through a darkened window into each boudoir.

In one they will see fine elegantly dressed young men playing at cards, music, etc. – in others athletic men, wrestling or bathing, in a perfect state of nudity ... Having fixed upon one she should like to enjoy, the lady has only to ring for the chambermaid, call her to the window, point out the object, and he is brought to the boudoir ... A lady of seventy or eighty years of age can at pleasure enjoy a fine robust youth of twenty ...

Temples of pleasure

In St James's Street, Miss Fawkland set up three adjoining temples of pleasure, each containing 12 girls. In the Temple of Aurora – which Fawkland called the 'first noviciate of pleasure' – the girls were between 11 and 16. They were well fed, well dressed and taught to read, write and sew by two governesses. They also attended dancing classes and were introduced to an extensive library of erotica to inflame their senses.

However, they were watched closely and not allowed to masturbate. Nor were they allowed to leave. They did receive visitors, though. These were men over 60 who Miss Fawkland had satisfied herself were impotent. They included Lord Buckingham and Lord Cornwallis.

At the age of 16, the girls were transferred to the Temple of Flora. Because of their extensive erotic education in the Temple of Aurora, they were 'indescribably sensual'. All the gifts and money they collected were pooled and divided evenly. Unusually, Miss Fawkland took only a small cut and she allowed girls to leave if they wanted to. As the conditions in the Temple of Aurora were so much better than at other houses, she had no difficulty replacing them. Clients included the playwright Richard Brinsley Sheridan, the novelist Tobias Smollett, Lord Bolingbroke and Lord Hamilton.

The third temple was known as the Temple of Mysteries. What went on there was secret. It seems to have catered for more esoteric tastes and girls from the other two temples – or from any other brothel – were not allowed to enter.

Massage parlours

In the nineteenth century, 'massage institutes' were popular fronts for prostitution. Other houses offered 'manicure', 'magneto-therapy', 'sexual friction baths' and all sorts of other spurious therapies. Under these seemingly respectable guises, their practitioners advertised. In the journal *Society*, a Miss Des- mond offered 'manicure and treatment for Rheumatism from two until eight'. The ad does not reveal how she is qualified, but mentions she was 'late of 11a, Air Street, Regent Street'.

Meanwhile Augusta Montgomery promised 'rheumatism and neuralgia, nerve and insomnia treatment' at the 'School of Modern Discipline', which sort of gives the game away.

The National Vigilance Society

Ever vigilant, the National Vigilance Society sent 27-year-old writer of religious music George Frederick Robertson to investigate. And they got their money's worth. Robertson's reports confirmed their fears 'as regards the practices universally carried on in the treatment of rheumatism, manicure, chiropody, etc. ... I strongly suspect that women of shameless life are engaged in these practices.'

A certain Madame M, for example, was

> very artful but anyone willing to spend a pound or more there can get there any amount of beastliness and immorality. The girls practise all the genital perversions known, such as flagellation, penis-sucking, etc., described by Dr Jacobus's Ethnology of the Sixth Sense and Genital Laws; Madame herself being a 'taker-on' and a whore of no mean capacity.

Robertson also reported seeing ten naked girls in one massage establishment 'prostituting their various charms for all sorts of purposes'. This was, plainly, a temptation Robertson could not resist. Not only did he succumb, he used his position with the society to extort money from the girls. Eventually he was charged with demanding money with menaces from Miss Janette Aspeaslagh. In court, she testified that, after calling on her and giving her money, Robertson said he was a 'detective' and threatened to go to the police.

She was forced to return the 10 shillings (50p) he had paid her, 'although', the court report said, 'he had had carnal connection with this lady several times'.

A number of clergymen appeared as character witnesses for the defence. Nevertheless the jury found Robertson guilty and he was sentenced to four years' penal servitude, as the judge had no doubt that 'the prisoner had been carrying on this nefarious and abominable traffic in going to these houses and indulging himself in immorality and then demanding money from unfortunate women, for some time past'.

The Balneopathic Institute

The Balneopathic Institute at 120 Marylebone was run by a black man named James Davis and offered treatments for rheumatism, gout and neuralgia by hot-air baths, massage, discipline and the like. Exactly what went on came to light when one of the girls who worked there complained of bodily injury. She was Davis's girlfriend and had supported him for two years from her earnings as a dressmaker before he had started the institute.

The other girls there, the plaintiff said, had been domestic servants of the defendant 'against whom he behaved immorally'. They were then taken on as attendants and provided with a skimpy uniform. Men who came to the institute were left alone with the girls and the plaintiff herself had been forced to accommodate the demands made of her.

Flagellation was the order of the day. When Davis was arrested, he was found to have a letter in his possession that read,

> Dear Mr Davis, I cannot come to you today as I have another appointment ... I should like to see you and will come tomorrow at the same time. Have whips ready, one for me and one each for the two Spanish women. One shilling for each stroke.

Gentlemen, apparently, paid a large entrance fee to see the attendants being beaten. The plaintiff herself said that she had been whipped unmercifully by the defendant.

CHAPTER EIGHT

Medical Matters

HE EARLIEST ENGLISH medical books mention diseases of the genital organs. In the fifteenth century they mention swellings, cankers and running sores. These are lumped together under a disease they called the 'burning'. But worse was to come.

Syphilis

A more deadly strain of venereal disease we now know as syphilis arrived in England in 1496, probably brought home by English mercenaries who had fought under Charles VIII when the French king invaded Naples in 1496. The disease was then known as the Spanish pox, later the French pox, though the people of Bristol called it *morbus Burdigalensis*, believing that it had been introduce from Bordeaux in 1498.

Because of the expansion of British trading activities and the number of people visiting London – then the biggest city in the world – syphilis took a hold on the capital. In Elizabethan times, the royal physician William Clowes noted that 'among every twenty diseased persons that are taken in [at St Bartholomew's Hospital] fifteen of them have the pox'.

The French pox

In 1729, *Satan's Harvest Home* said

> The greatest evil that attends this vice, or could befall mankind, is the propagation of that infectious disease call'd the French pox, which in two centuries has made such an incredible havoc all over Europe. In these kingdoms, it so seldom fails to attend whoring, nowadays mistaken for gallantry and politeness ... Men give it to their wives, women to their husbands, or perhaps their children; they to their nurses, and the nurses again to other children; so that no age, sex or condition can be entirely free from the infection.

Indeed the author pointed out that not to have the pox was considered a 'mark of ungentility and ill-breeding' and anyone who failed to catch it was considered a boor.

The Lock Hospital in Harrow Road, which specialised in treating the disease, was founded in 1746. Between 1747 and 1836, 44,973 sufferers were admitted. And syphilis was no respecter of age. Though many cases went unreported and untreated, 2,700 cases of venereal disease were diagnosed in children aged 11–16 between 1827 and 1835. In one hospital a woman and her five daughters of 8, 9, 11, 12 and 13 were all found to have the disease.

By the last decades of the nineteenth century, venereal disease was so common that 'health bureaux' were established in

London and other English ports. The prostitutes were examined by doctors and given a certificate if they did not have the disease.

Prevention

The better brothels had their girls regularly inspected for the pox by a doctor and any showing symptoms were rejected. There were, of course, condoms, which would reduce the risk of catching it. But, as always, these were unpopular with men and, in the eighteenth century, it became fashionable to carry a little box of grease around. This was smeared on the glans before intercourse and thought to be prophylactic.

Cure

In the late eighteenth century, it was widely believed that the cure for venereal disease was to have sex with someone unaffected. This led to the rape of a large number of underage girls.

Condoms

The use of condoms was established in England during the reign of Charles II. Originally made out of fish bladder or the appendix of lambs, they were said to have been invented by a

Dr Conton. However, in the seventeenth century, no doctor of that name has been traced. Condoms were, in fact, invented by the Italian anatomist Gabriello Fallopio, who gave his name to the Fallopian tubes. They were made from fish skins and aimed to guard against venereal diseases. It is thought that one of Charles II's courtiers, a Colonel Condum or Cundum, brought some with him from the Continent when he returned at the Restoration in 1660.

It may be that an improvement was made to Fallopio's original design by an English doctor by using animal skin. They were then used for contraception as well as to curb the transmission of disease. In his memoirs, Casanova mentions 'the little shields which the English have invented to keep the fair sex from worrying'.

But the 1840s, they were made out of vulcanised rubber and came in tins with pictures of Gladstone or Queen Victoria on the lid. And even in Victorian times the 'stimulant condom' with spines or points to increase the woman's pleasure were available.

Other means of contraception

The so-called 'occlusive pessary' was available in Victorian times. This consisted of a hemisphere of rubber supported on a steel ring that was inserted into the vagina before intercourse. Apart from the difficulty of putting this in place, it was liable to be displaced during intercourse and often caused irritation. However, a device made with waterproof cambric was said to be less irritating.

A 'duplex occlusive pessary' was also available. This had a double wall. The outer one was perforated to allow the boric acid in between to seep out, killing the spermatozoa.

Then there was Gall's 'balloon occlusive pessary', which consisted of a soft elastic rubber disc surrounded by a thin-walled rubber ring. Once in position, the ring was inflated using a compressible rubber ball and tubing. Hardly the most romantic of beginnings.

By the end of the nineteenth century, there were over 100 kinds of mechanical device available, from a simple stopper to 'a patent thrashing machine', which was said to look like a water wheel and could be worn only under the largest crinoline. Whether this was supposed to discourage a potential lover or induce an abortion is not known.

There was also the 'Venus apparatus'. A small rubber ball filled with 'Venus powder' was connected to a larger ball by tubing. The smaller ball was inserted into the vagina. At the moment of ejaculation the woman squeezed the larger ball, which expelled the Venus powder within.

There were also antiseptic 'security sponges' that were so unreliable that they were known in the medical profession as 'insecurity sponges'. Otherwise there were Hollweg's 'obturator', 'security ovals' containing boric acid, quinine or citric acid, 'little vaginal plugs', 'salus ovula', Kamp's anti-conceptional cotton-wool plugs, Hüter's vaginal insufflator 'for the malthusian', Noffke's tampon-speculum, 'spermath-anaton' pastilles and Weissl's 'preservative', which was a combination of a speculum and a rubber disc with a steel spring and a cotton-wool plug impregnated with a chemical.

By the late nineteenth century, the most common variety of contraception – and probably the most unreliable – was the douche. This was performed with a syringe called a 'Lady's friend'. The rhythm method, *coitus interruptus* and *coitus reservatus* were known at practised. And apparently 'maiden pills' invented by a French doctor were also in use.

Abortion and its alternatives

Abortion was widely practised in Victorian times. Even though it was against the law, clinics offering such a service advertised discreetly in the newspapers. In the 1870s, it was reported that there was a doctor in the West End who, at any one time, had six or seven girls waiting their turn to be operated on. For the most part, it was said, these young women were 'connected with the theatre'. The fee for the operation was £5 – £300 at today's prices. Yew needles were used.

Otherwise, from the eighteenth century onwards, there were a large number of nursing homes where young women could have babies in secret. The baby could then be adopted. These places advertised in the newspapers and through handbills distributed in the streets.

Midwifery

In 1618, a Miss Willughby, a midwife, wanted her father Dr Percy Willughby's opinion on a critical case. But the doctor could not openly enter the room where the confinement was taking place.

'At my daughter's request, I crawled in on hands and knees,' he said.

For the following 150 years, the practice continued until, finally, male doctors were allowed to deliver babies.

Male birth pangs

In 1865, the practice of couvade, or 'hatching' was identified in primitive societies by the Victorian anthropologist E.B. Tylor. It was essentially a reversal of roles between men and women during the process of childbirth. When the women felt the first pangs of labour, her husband would take to his bed, sometimes donning her clothes before lying down. The woman continued her normal work until the actual birth, and resumed her tasks a few hours after. Meanwhile, the man affected to experience the pains of childbirth and stayed in his bed for days, sometimes weeks.

In *Folk-Medicine*, published in 1883, William Black pointed out that the practice of couvade had not entirely vanished from the United Kingdom, as then constituted. 'In Ireland the tradition remains,' he wrote. 'The husband does not indeed pretend to suffer the pains of labour, but the nurses boast that they possess the power of transferring the sufferings to him or to any other person they please.'

CHAPTER NINE

French Kissing

HEN THE NORMANS invaded England in 1066, they brought with them the French ways of love. They introduced widespread pederasty. William Rufus, son of William the Conqueror, made little secret of his preferences. The Norman kings were followed by the Plantagenets, a French family, and pederasty received another kick up the backside during the Crusades. Richard the Lionheart, old England's greatest hero, preferred the company of his rough crusaders to that of his queen, leaving his marriage unconsummated. And, famously, Edward II was despatched with a red hot poker up 'those parts in which he had been wont to take his vicious pleasures'.

Secret favours

Women were particularly influential in the French political culture brought over by the Normans. In his *History of Women* (1779), William Alexander said that councils of state were often held in the lady's bedroom while the lady herself was in bed and decisions were reached 'commonly by promises of secret favours'.

In the houses of the great, he said, apartments were provided for the women, who were employed in various kinds of needlework, 'and the name given to these apartments, in consequence of the use that was made of them, came in time to be synonymous to that of a brothel'. Even the clergy were not ashamed to have inscriptions over the doors of these apartments, signifying their use, and Cardinal Wolsey, over a door of a particular part of his palace, had the words in Latin, THE HOUSE OF THE WHORES OF MY LORD THE CARDINAL.

The king's pleasure

Those medieval English kings who favoured women kept a number of them and there would be a room in the palace bearing the inscription, ROOM OF THE KING'S PROSTITUTES.

Henrys I and II lived in open polygamy and had more illegitimate children than legitimate ones. Henry IV, the 'usurper', was a notorious lecher. His son, the great warrior Henry V, also 'fervently followed the service of Venus as well as of Mars'.

Henry VI was more prudish. On one occasion, when a troupe of half-naked dancing girls was laid on to entertain him, Henry ran from the room crying: 'Fy, fy, for shame.' He himself was impotent. When his wife Margaret of Anjou announced that she was pregnant, he collapsed. Court gossip had it that the child was the bastard of the Duke of Somerset and the scandal surrounding this helped Edward IV to seize the throne.

Edward was 'licentious in the extreme', according to contemporary reports. However, he took no woman by force, it was said. He overcame all by money and promises, and, having conquered them, he dismissed them. Be that as it may, he did threaten them. He tried to rape the widowed Elizabeth Woodville at knifepoint. Only when she said that she would rather die than have him did he promise to marry her.

But Edward's mistress Jane Shore was more influential. At a time when the ducking stool was used to punish promiscuous women, she escaped and the couplet 'The reason why she is not duck'd, / Because by Caesar she is fucked' circulated. A reward of £1,000 was offered for the name of the author, but no one dared claim it.

After Edward died, Jane Shore became the mistress of Elizabeth Woodville's oldest son, then William Lord Hastings. Richard III had her arrested and forced to do public penance as a harlot. She died a beggar 1527 and it is thought that Shoreditch in London is named after her.

Clerical celibacy

When the Council of Piacenza outlawed priests' marriages in 1095, the clergy of the church in England made it clear that they did not wish to remain single.

Pope Honorius II sent Cardinal John of Crema to England as papal legate in September 1126 to denounce the concubines of priests. The pope instructed him to declare that it was a horrible sacrilege on the body of Christ that mass should be performed by a man who had just left the bed of a harlot. The cardinal assembled a great council in London and, against much opposition, passed a canon threatening the demotion of all clergy who would not give up their wives or courtesans. Then he celebrated a solemn mass and the assembly dispersed.

But the English clergy knew full well what their Italian brethren were like. They kept a careful watch on the cardinal's lodgings. That night, a muffled figure was seen creeping out of the back door. They followed it down the street to the house of a well-known prostitute. The figure knocked and entered. After 10 minutes or so, a couple of English clergymen burst in to find the Cardinal *nudatus usque ad unguem* – naked to his fingernails – with a 'fayre ladye' in a similar state of undress. After raising a toast to the Cardinal's appropriately scarlet face, they left him to get on with his business.

The events of the evening 'brought no small scandal on the Church'. It proved the end of John of Crema's campaign against the wives and concubines of the English clergy. The Cardinal was packed off back to Rome with instructions to tell the pope to put his own house in order first.

Lemmans

According to John Foxe's *Acts and Monuments of the Christian Martyrs*, the English clergy kept a hundred thousand harlots before the Reformation. They were known as lemmans, a corruption of *l'amante*, the French word for lover. They were also notorious for seducing women in the confessional.

When a priest seduced the daughter of a nobleman and killed her father, Henry II demanded that he be handed over to the secular authorities, but the Archbishop of Canterbury Thomas à Becket refused, saying that the man had already been punished by being suspended from duty and it was not right that a person be punished twice for the same crime.

Sin tax

King John imposed a 'sin tax' on the clergy's wives and concubines – then known as *focarie* or hearthmates. His men would seize them and force the priests to buy them back at exorbitant prices. But later John was forced to guarantee the freedom of the church in England in Magna Carta. Ironically, he was made to sign the charter by the barons, who were fed up with his making free with their wives and daughters. John took a less charitable view of his wife's sexual indulgence. When

Isabella of Angoulème took a lover, John had him and his two accomplices killed and their bodies draped over her bed.

Co-ed convents

In 1148, St Gilbert of Sempringham established an order known as the Gilbertines, the only native English monastic order. The unusual thing about the Gilbertines was that monks and nuns lived together in the same complex. In church there was a high wall so that the monks and nuns could not see each other at their devotions, but both could hear the preaching.

It was asking for trouble. The French writer Gabriel d'Emilianne said that in a short time Gilbert 'got thirteen cloisters built in which seven hundred monks and eleven hundred nuns lived together, separated only by the thickness of wall. This hermaphroditic order, consisting of both sexes, soon produced worthy fruit. For these holy virgins, nearly all of them, became pregnant.'

This led to the following verse to be written:

Though some are barren does, yet others,
By friars help, proving teeming mothers.
When all to such lewdness run
All's covered under the name of nun.
The abbess in honour as she excells,
Her belly, too, more often swells.
If any she proves barren still
Age is in fault, but not her will.

But there were tales of tragedy too. A girl had been placed in the priory at Watton in Yorkshire by the Archbishop of York. As she grew up she found she had no real vocation and became intimate with one of the lay brothers and fell pregnant. Her lover escaped but was caught. The nuns then forced the girl to cut off the man's genitals, then stuffed them in the girl's throat. She was kept in shackles until the archbishop visited. Then, it was said, the evidence of her pregnancy disappeared and her chains fell away.

The Gilbertines' Sempringham Priory fell in the diocese of the Bishop of Lincoln. He developed a novel test to see if the nuns were fooling around. When he visited a convent he would fondle their breasts to see how they reacted.

CHAPTER TEN

The Torrid Tudors

LTHOUGH HENRY TUDOR married and stayed faithful to his wife for political reasons – his marriage united the warring houses of Lancaster and York – his son did not follow suit. But Henry VIII was not the legendary stud that history has made out. Medical records show that he was impotent in at least two of his marriages – those to Anne of Cleves and Catherine Parr.

He failed to satisfy Catherine Howard, who comprehensively cuckolded him. Anne Boleyn was also accused of infidelity. And his marriages to Catherine of Aragon and Anne Boleyn were incestuous by the standards of the time. Catherine was the widow of his older brother Arthur and Henry had child by Anne's sister Mary.

Then, after the reign of the sickly Edward VI, the throne was occupied by a series of women.

Kissing

In the sixteenth century, foreigners found it shocking that it was customary in England for ladies to reward their dance partners with a kiss. What intrigued them even more was the habit of women to kiss each other on the lips. One Elizabethan couplet ran, 'Were kisses all the joys of bed, / One woman would another wed.' Indeed, women of fashion, such as Lady Penelope Rich, made themselves available to women and men.

Topless queen

According to the French ambassador, Queen Elizabeth I was a bit of a flasher. She liked to appear in court wearing only a diaphanous gown. Even in old age she let the dress gape, exposing her wrinkled breasts. The image she tried to project was that of the nurturing mother of the nation.

It should be noted that Elizabeth was no virgin, despite the fact Virginia was named after her. Her stepfather Thomas Seymour certainly made an assault on her maidenhead. When she was queen there was talk of numerous suitors, including Lord Robert Dudley and, later, his stepson the Earl of Essex.

In 1559, she asked Sir John Mason to instruct the House of Commons to erect a marble stone to declare that she lived and died a virgin. Even though Elizabeth is known as the Virgin Queen, no such monument was ever erected. During her lifetime, Elizabeth herself complained of being 'of barren stock'. How could she have known that if she had not slept with a man?

A tree trembler

At one time Sir Walter Raleigh's name was linked to Elizabeth's, but he blew his chances of becoming king – or a least the royal consort – when he seduced a lady of the bedchamber named Elizabeth Throckmorton. The diarist John Aubrey immortalised the encounter, describing how Sir Walter

> loved a wench well and, one time, getting up one of the maids of honour against a tree in a wood ('twas his first lady) who seemed at first boarding to be fearful of her honour, and modest, she cried, 'Sweet Sir Walter, what do you me ask? Will you undo me? Nay sweet Sir Walter!' At last, as the danger and pleasure at the same time grew higher, she cried in the ecstasy 'Swisser Swatter! Swisser Swatter!' She proved with child.

Royal treasures

Elizabeth I's court was full of sexual intrigue. Maid of honour Lucie Morgan left to become a bawd in St John's Street, Clerkenwell, under the name Lucy Negro and ended up in Bridewell. Two other maids of honour were kicked out for sexual misconduct and had to take refuge with Lady Dorothy Stafford. Few of the maids were thought to be virgins when they turned up at court.

Then there was Sir William Knollys, treasurer to the royal household and thought to be the model for Malvolio in Shakespeare's *Twelfth Night*. At court, he was lodged next to a room where 'some of the ladies and maids of honour used to frisk and hey about'. Unable to sleep one night, Knollys, naked except for his spectacles, marched in carrying a copy of a book by the Italian pornographer Pietro Aretino, plainly prepared for more than a reading.

CHAPTER ELEVEN

The Saucy Stuarts

LIZABETH I WAS SUCCEEDED by James VI of Scotland, the first of the ill-fated Stuarts. He became James I of England and shocked everyone with his outrageously camp behaviour when he arrived in London. Despite having seven children by his queen, Anne of Denmark, he had numerous male lovers. They were given titles and favourable marriages were arranged for them when his fancy turned elsewhere. James seems to have shared a lover, the Duke of Buckingham, with his son Charles.

Dynasty

After Charles I was beheaded in 1649, England lived for 11 years under the Puritan rule of Oliver Cromwell. Then Charles II – known as 'Old Rowley' after a randy goat tethered on the palace green – was restored to the throne. The Restoration began a period of unbridled sexual licence.

Charles once confided to the French ambassador that his brother the Duke of York – who succeeded him as James II –

had had more lovers than the two of them put together. However, as a penance imposed by priests for the good of his soul, he slept only with ugly women. James had two daughters, who shared girlfriends in their youth. The elder, Mary, had the good fortune to marry William of Orange, who seldom bothered her, as his interest lay in other men.

In the Glorious Revolution, James was deposed and replaced by William and Mary. James, who was finally defeated at the Battle of the Boyne, blamed his ill-fortune on 'letting myself go too much in the love of women'.

When William died, he was succeeded by Mary's sister, Queen Anne, who caused a scandal when she replaced her aristocratic lover, Sarah Churchill, with the lowly Abigail Hill, who was described in a scurrilous ballad of 1708 as a 'dirty chamber maid'.

Restoration revels

In the Restoration, English sexual life reached a new peak as the Stuart court returned from the Continent bringing the amorous ways of the French and Spaniards with it. The tone was set by Charles II himself, who spent his first night back in London on 29 May 1660 in the arms of – or, more accurately, between the legs of – Barbara Palmer, Lady Castlemaine.

When Charles's queen, Catherine of Braganza, arrived from Portugal the following year, Charles was still deeply embroiled with his young mistress. Pepys recorded,

> The King dined with my Lady Castlemaine, and supped, every day and night last week. And the night that the

bonfires were made for joy of the Queen's arrival, the King was there; but there was no fire at her door, though at all the rest of the doors almost in the street; which was much observed. And that the King and she did send for a pair of scales and weighed one another; and she, being with child, was said to be the heaviest.

Royal threesomes

Lady Castlemaine had an insatiable appetite and slept with numerous courtiers, including Charles's illegitimate son the Duke of Monmouth and John Churchill, who went on to become the Duke of Marlborough, victor of the Battle of Blenheim. But she was a jealous lover. When she saw that the King's roving eye had turned to the beauteous Miss Stewart, she took her to bed herself, then set up a royal threesome. According to Pepys, one night Lady Castlemaine and Miss Stewart

> began a frolique that they two must be married and married they were, with ring and all other ceremonies of church service, and ribbands and a sack-posset in bed and flinging the stocking. But in the close, it is said that my Lady Castlemaine, who was the bridegroom, rose, and the King came and took her place.

The two women then became deadly rivals. When Charles bought the Queen a new carriage, Lady Castlemaine thought that it would show off her charms when she rode in Hyde Park and asked to borrow it. Miss Stewart thought the same and asked to borrow the carriage on the very same day. Lady Castle-maine, who was pregnant at the time, threatened to give birth prematurely if she did not get her way. Miss Stewart assured the King that she would effectively ensure that she never got in that condition if he did not comply with her wishes. She won the day, the carriage and the King.

More mistresses

Charles II went on to have countless other mistresses including Louise de Keroualle, an agent of the french king, Louis XIV. After a 'mock marriage' at Euston Hall in October 1672, the diarist John Evelyn recorded, 'The fair lady was bedded one of these nights and the stocking flung after the manner of a married bride.' Afterwards she was made Duchess of Portsmouth.

Being French and Catholic, Louise was far from popular. Above the door of her sumptuous apartments in the recently refurbished Palace of Whitehall appeared the sign:

WITHIN THIS PLACE A BED'S APPOINTED

FOR A FRENCH BITCH AND GOD'S ANOINTED.

The King's most famous mistress was the former child-prostitute-cum-orange-seller-cum-actress Nell Gwyn, who won the King from fellow actress Moll Davis by dosing Moll's sweetmeats with a powerful laxative on the eve of an assignation with the King and stepping into the breach.

One day a coach approached the royal apartment. Thinking it carried Louise de Keroualle, a noisy mob surrounded it, denouncing her as a Catholic whore. In fact, the coach was carrying Nell Gwyn, who stuck her head out of the window and shouted, 'Pray good people be civil, I am the Protestant whore.'

The beauties of the court

When the Stuart court returned to England, it bought some notable Frenchmen with it. These included the amateur moralist Charles de Marguetel de Saint Denis, Seigneur de Saint-Évremond and Count Grammont. In 1713, his brother-in-law Anthony Hamilton published *Memoirs of the life of Count Grammont: containing in particular the amorous intrigues of the Court of England in the reign of King Charles II*, which painted a seductive picture of court life:

> At court, all was happiness and pleasure, refinement and splendour such as may be called forth by a prince of gentle and noble character. Beauties sought only to be enchanting, men tried to please and everyone made the most of their natural gifts. Some of them distinguished themselves by the grace of their dancing, some by the magnificence of their appearance and some by their wit, but most by their love affairs and very few of them by their faithfulness.

Hamilton was also fond of the revealing clothing the ladies wore and the ease with which they shed it. The bathing negligées of the court ladies, he said, 'served only to exhibit their charms without being actually indecent'; and of Lady Castlemaine's rival Miss Stewart he said, 'Indeed, with a little skill, I don't think it would be difficult to get her, all unsuspecting, completely unclothed.'

In Restoration court, women openly discussed their lovers' physical prowess while men described the intimate joys of their mistresses' bodies. And it was not uncommon for men to hand their wives on to their friends 'to make what use they liked of them, as Mr Cooke did to Sir William Baron,' wrote one Restoration wife.

Clever women

The Restoration saw the rise of a number of women writers. Aphra Behn (1640–89) was the first woman in England to make her living by her pen. Her work so accurately reflected the spirit of her times that she is often described as England's first female pornographer.

Another racy writer was Mary de la Riviere, who caused a scandal by bigamously marrying her cousin, the MP John Manley.

Unashamed of her lax morals, she said, 'It was to the interest of the women to make everyone fall in love with them, and the mere indifference of a young man was looked upon as an insult. The King, by this own example, encouraged this view.'

As she grew older she used her pen for satirical effect. In 1709, she published *The Atalantis of Mrs Manley, or a secret*

Report on the most distinguished Persons in England, which exposed the vices of Whig ministers, and helped bring down the government.

'People nowadays do not love for the sake of love, but chiefly on account of its use and profit to them,' she rued.

And in 1711, she succeeded Jonathan Swift as editor of the *Examiner*.

Masks

As well as writing plays, women appeared on stage for the first time during the reign of Charles II. In the audience, though, women hid their faces behind masks, so they could watch bawdy plays incognito. But, when Queen Anne came to the throne, she banned this practice. Prostitutes had taken to using the same device to slip unnoticed into theatres and solicit for trade between acts.

Queen Anne also banned 'persons of what quality soever' going 'behind the scenes or upon the stage either before or during the acting of a play' as most of the actresses were also prostitutes. They watched for suitable customers from the stage, attempting to inflame them with explicit acts on stage, and, afterwards, took them to the brothels that grew up near the theatres.

Drury taverns

Married women who sought a little amorous adventure also wore masks. It meant that they could visit haunts of ill repute without being recognised, particularly so-called Drury taverns that had sprung up near the theatres in the reign of Charles II. The last of them, the White Lion in Wych Street, was closed in May 1724.

For some time, masked orgies had been going on in the upstairs dance hall in the guise of a concert. When the constables finally raided it, they found common prostitutes mixing with the rich merchants' wives, ladies of rank and their daughters. The prostitutes could not believe that they were in such good company, while the high-class ladies were shocked at the low-class circle they were moving in.

The ladies were given a caution and sent home. The prostitutes were taken to the Bridewell. Later, both ladies and gentlemen of quality turned out to see 'ladies of the town cooled by the cat-o'-nine-tails'. This often occurred in the room next to the court and folding doors were opened so the whole court could witness the punishment. One poor woman who had no one to speak for her 'was forced to show her tender back and tempting bubbies to the grave sages of the august assembly, who were moved by her modest mien, together with the whiteness of her skin, to give her but a gentle correction'.

A debilitating revenge

According to the writer Mrs Manley (see 'Clever women' above), deceived husbands sought to take their revenge 'without poison or iron'. When Lord Southesk suspected his promiscuous wife had been procured by Lord Falmouth for the Marquis de Flamarens, he visited notorious stews to pick up

> the most disgusting of all diseases. But he only half succeeded in revenging himself because, after he had undergone the most drastic treatment to rid himself of the disease, he was to have the gift returned to him by his wife, for she carried on no more intercourse with the man for whom the present was intended.

The Marquis de Flamarens, it seems, escaped with nothing worse than a broken heart.

Slumming it

The aristocrats of the day loved slumming it. Bishop Burnet complained, 'The court in those days took part in the most licentious masquerades. The King and Queen, ladies and courtiers, went about in disguise, entered houses of unknown people and danced there, making bad jokes.'

The diarist John Evelyn said that ladies of rank frequented taverns where even courtesans would never set foot. 'But you will be even more astonished to hear that they passed their large glasses round,' he wrote, 'drank each other's health, danced to the music of the violin, freely distributed kisses, and called this a decent form of amusement.'

This would not astonish the Monsieur de Cominges, the French ambassador, who reported that people of rank in England indulged themselves to excess in taverns and brothels – 'even ladies of very distinguished families would accompany their gallants to such places'.

One-time court favourite the Earl of Rochester moved from Westminster into the City, living under an assumed name to get to know the merchants there, attend their parties and enjoy their wives. Meanwhile, two ladies of the court, Miss Price and Miss Frances Jennings, disguised themselves as orange girls and plied their trade outside the theatres.

Blasphemous clubs

'Blasphemous' societies and clubs originated in the Restoration and specialised in 'debauchery and profaneness'. Among them were the 'Ballers' – young blades who gathered at the brothel of 'Lady Bennet and her ladies', where there was nude dancing and 'all the roguish things in the world'.

The Bold Bucks adopted the 'flaming lust' of their animal namesakes and they took as their motto 'blind and bold love'. A contemporary observer said, 'They attempt all females of their own species promiscuously – grandmothers and mothers, as well as daughters; even their own sisters fear their violence, and fly their privacies.'

Another club, in Queen Anne's reign, called themselves the Tumblers. They specialised in turning women upside down and standing them on their heads. It must be remembered that, at that time, women wore no underwear.

Restoration procuresses

After the end of the Puritan era, procuresses had their work cut out. Most famous among them were Mother Moreley, Mother Ross and Mother Bennett. Mother Beaulieu achieved notoriety when she sued the Archbishop of Rheims, who had placed several orders with her, but had not paid for them. Prostitution was rapidly becoming an international trade.

Charles II himself patronised a procuress named Madame Creswell. From her home in Clerkenwell, she sent agents out throughout England and France soliciting pretty girls. When the City of London closed down a number of brothels, an impertinent pamphlet circulated, ostensibly signed by Madame Creswell. It was entitled 'Petition of the poor Whore to the most serene, illustrious, august and excellent Lady of pleasure, Countess of Castlemaine', and asked for her support for 'a trade wherein your Ladyship has great experience'. Lady Castlemaine was livid, and another satirist thoughtfully penned a 'Gracious Answer' on her behalf.

Highwaymen

High-born ladies fell for a gallant highwaymen named Claude Duval, a Frenchman who had once been page to the Duke of Richmond. He attacked travellers on their way through Holloway from Islington to Highgate.

In one coach he stopped there was a lady carrying £400. He took £100 and told her she could keep the other £300 if she would dance a coranto with him on the heath.

Like other highwaymen, he spent his free time in the pubs of St Giles's, where prostitutes held orgies in the cellars. One pub there famously advertised that you could get: 'Drunk for a penny, dead drunk for tuppence, straw for nothing.'

Duval must have paid tuppence, as he was caught sleeping off a skinful of sweet wine in the Hole-in-the-Wall pub in Chandos Street. Ladies of the highest rank visited him in jail. They got up a petition and the king would have pardoned him had not the judge in the case, Sir William Morton, not threatened to resign.

After he was hanged, Duval lay in state in the Tangiers Tavern, St Giles's, and was buried in the middle aisle of St Paul's Church in Covent Garden 'to the great grief of the women'. Later, a street named 'Devil's Way' in Lower Holloway was renamed 'Duval's Lane'.

Hyde and seek

Charles II's younger brother, the Duke of York – later James II – had tried to keep his marriage to his sister Mary's maid of honour, Anne Hyde, secret, particularly from her father, Charles's prudish Lord Chancellor, Edward Hyde. However, by the time the court returned to England, Anne was already carrying his child.

James then went through a conventional wedding ceremony to secure his pregnant wife's position, causing the Earl of Sandwich to remark, 'That he that doth get a wench with child and marries her afterward, it is as if a man should shit in his hat and then clap it upon his head.'

Both his mother Queen Henrietta-Maria and his sister Mary, who was then the Princess of Orange, expressed outrage at James's marriage to a commoner, with Mary declaring that she would never accept as a sister-in-law a former maid of honour who had once stood as a servant behind her chair. And Henrietta-Maria and Mary rushed over from the Continent, intent on preventing dishonour on the Crown.

When Anne's father the Lord Chancellor heard, he ordered that she be taken to the Tower of London immediately to await execution. James, meanwhile, insisted that, unless Anne was officially acknowledged as his wife, he would leave the kingdom and spend the rest of his life abroad. But soon he had second thoughts. Anne's plain looks and dumpy figure had not been enhanced by her pregnancy, and he began to pursue the many young beauties who had flocked to the Restoration court.

Then, in a callous attempt to rid himself of Anne, he got five of his friends to claim to be the father of the child. James even denied that he had ever married the woman, publicly or privately – though he had done so, twice.

On 22 October 1660, Anne gave birth to a sickly boy. Throughout her pregnancy, she doggedly maintained that James was her husband and the father of her child. Eventually, the King took pity on her. He quelled the scandal by insisting that James marry her. The duke's five friends were forced to retract their allegations and on 21 December 1660 James publicly admitted the marriage, though it did not stop him fooling around.

Anne got her revenge in the end. Although her son died, she later gave birth to two healthy girls, Mary and Anne. When she died, James, by then a declared Catholic, married Mary of Modena, who was both royal and Catholic. When she gave birth to a daughter, the idea of a Catholic heir was more than the Protestants in Parliament could stand. They invited the Protestant William of Orange to become king. James was ousted and Anne Hyde's daughters in turn – first Mary, William's wife, then Anne – became Queen of England.

CHAPTER TWELVE

The Gorgeous Georgians

HE GEORGIANS WERE just as bad as the saucy Stuarts. George I left his wife imprisoned in a castle in Hanover, after having her lover murdered, and turned up in England with two mistresses – one tall and thin, the other fat. They were known as the 'maypole and the elephant'. George II regularly returned to Hanover to spend time with his numerous mistresses there. This did not escape public attention. A broken-down nag was let loose on the streets of London, with a sign around its head which announced: 'I am the King's Hanoverian Equipage going to fetch his Majesty and his whore to England.' And someone pinned a note to the door of St James's Palace that read,

Lost or strayed out of this house, a man who has left a wife and six children on the parish; whoever will give any tidings of him to the churchwardens of St James's Parish, so he may be got again, shall receive four shillings and sixpence. N.B. This reward will not be increased, nobody judging him to deserve a Crown.

George III tried to clean up his act, but one of the symptoms of his madness was erotomania. His heir, who became the prince regent and later George IV, illegally married the twice-divorced Mrs Maria Fitzherbert, then entered the disastrous marriage to Caroline of Brunswick-Lüneburg, resulting in the 'Delicate Investigation'. Afterwards, he continued to take mistresses from among the highest in the land.

A family affair

George III passed the Royal Marriages Act in an attempt to curb the excesses of his children. It failed. The Duke of Clarence, who became William IV, spent much of his youth frequenting whorehouses in the West Indies, where he enjoyed sex and flogging, and caused a scandal when he returned from Jamaica with his Caribbean concubine 'Wowski'. Then he set up home with an actress called Mrs Jordan, abandoning her after she had had 10 children, to marry Princess Adelaide of Saxe-Coburg and Meiningen.

Prince Edward abandoned his mistress of 25 years' standing to marry, briefly, Princess Victoria of Leinigen and father the future Queen Victoria. Prince Ernest took as his mistress the twice-widowed Frederica of Mecklenburg-Strelitz, who was said to have murdered at least one of her husbands. Ernest is also thought to have had an incestuous affair with his sister Princess Sophia, committing all manner of sexual perversion in a mirrored room in St James's Palace. The resulting child was passed off as the progeny of an equerry 33 years Sophia's senior. Princess Augusta and Princess Amelia both secretly married their equerries, while Princess Elizabeth fell pregnant at the age of 16, marrying at 47.

Prince Augustus Frederick abandoned his wife and children, then married a grocer's widow, while Prince Adolphus lived openly in Germany with his mistress. Needless to say, their behaviour set the standard for their subjects.

Demireps

In the eighteenth century, the ladies at court at least pretended to be modest and chaste, leading to the rise of the 'demirep'. *Rep* is the abbreviation of *reputation*, a thing, at the time, 'in constant danger of being lost or destroyed at tea-tables'.

Demireps had only half a reputation and preferred discreet sexual adventures to matrimony. Lady Mary Wortley Montagu lamented the trend:

I deplore the unpopularity of the married state, which is scorned by our young women these days, as it once was by men. Both sexes have discovered its inconveniences, and many feminine libertines may be found among young women of rank. No one is shocked to hear that 'Miss So-and-So, Maid of Honour, has got over her confinement nicely'.

Kitty Fisher

The eighteenth century also saw the rise of the celebrity courtesans. There was Kitty Fisher who 'distinguished herself by the unique manner in which she served the goddess Venus'.

A foreign observer noted that she was beautiful, intelligent, witty and greatly admired 'by all those who preferred the joys of sexual contact to any other pleasure in life'.

She charged 100 guineas (£105, or £12,000 today) a night and the Duke of York, brother of George III, was said to be among her patrons. Joshua Reynolds painted Kitty as Cleopatra, and her lovers came from the highest ranks. When she fell ill, six members of the House of Lords rushed to her bedside.

Her wealthy lovers meant that she enjoyed an extravagant lifestyle and tried to outdo all those around her. She once paid 20 guineas – the equivalent of £2,400 today – to eat strawberries in winter and had tea served in her box at the theatre during the performance. One French observer called her 'the English du Barry'.

Fanny Murray

Between 1735 and 1745, Fanny Murray was the toast of the town. Horace Walpole called her a 'famous beauty'. She counted among her lovers the wealthy John Spencer of Althorp and the dandy Richard 'Beau' Nash, and she posed nude with

Kitty Fisher for a painting. But her claim to fame came from John Wilkes's poem 'An Essay on Woman', which is dedicated to her and begins:

> Awake, my Fanny, leave all meaner things;
>   This morn shall prove what rapture swiving brings!
> Let us (since life can little more supply
>   Than just a few good fucks and then we die)

And so on, in much the same – and even more explicit – vein. Wilkes was a Member of Parliament. His 'Essay on Women' was ruled to have breached parliamentary privilege. He was expelled from Parliament and prosecuted for obscenity.

Like Kitty Fisher, Fanny Murray showed contempt for paltry sums of money. According to Horace Walpole, one night she was complaining that she had no money and her 'protector', Richard Atkins, gave her £20 – £2,200 today.

'Damn your twenty pounds,' she said. 'What does that signify?' And she put the note between two pieces of bread and ate it – appropriately, since she was once the mistress of Lord Sandwich.

Anna Bellamy

Born in 1731, the illegitimate daughter of Lord Tryawley, an old roué, the convent-educated actress Anna Bellamy – George Anne, as she was christened – was said to be 'one of the most amorous and lascivious women of her age'. Nevertheless, she had government ministers, ambassadors, generals and lords dining at her table every day. She also took an active role in court life and elections. However, she was denied respectability, as she always had a live-in lover. One of them was Charles James Fox, leader of the Whigs.

Although she was denied recognition in society, she enjoyed some measure of respectability, and even virtuous ladies of the highest rank maintained social intercourse with her and allowed their daughters to do the same.

Unashamedly, Anna Bellamy published five volumes of memoirs entitled *An Apology for the Life of George Anne Bellamy*, which was dedicated to the Prince of Wales. It was published in 1785 and went through three editions within the year.

Other literary ladies

The most famous memoirs came from the courtesan Harriette Wilson. She had slept with the prince regent, three prime ministers and most of the dandies of Mayfair. When she was writing her memoirs she asked her distinguished lovers for money if they wanted to be left out. The Duke of Wellington's response was, famously, 'Publish and be damned.'

In the same year as Anna Bellamy's published *Apology*, Mrs Harriot Errington went into print with *The Memoirs of Mrs. Harriot Er-g-n, containing Her Amours, Intrigues, Tête-à-têtes with the following well-known Characters, viz: Colonel M-n, Colonel T-l-n, Captain Sm-th* …, published in the wake of a scandalous adultery trial. The title page went on to mention 18 gentlemen, including seven military officers, two knights, one lord and a reverend. To that roster was added, 'also Coachmen, Footmen, Postillions, Butlers, Gardeners, Post-Chaise Boys, Grooms, Foot-boys, and many Others'.

Annabella Parsons, lover of the Duke of Grafton, was also celebrated in literature in 1769 in the *Intrigues à la Mode: Biographical Memoirs of the Late, Most Noble and Much Lamented Charles August Fitz-roy, Duke of Grafton, including some Remarkable Particulars in the Life of the Celebrated Miss Anna-bella, now Lady Maynard, with Amorous, Eccentric, and Whimsical Anecdotes of Several Other Beauties, and Famous Courtesans of the Time with Certain Persons of Distinction* – all that for just sixpence. It ran to just 21 pages and cost £30 in today's money.

Another memoirist was Harriot Mellon. A former actress, she advertised her wares on the stage in Drury Lane in *Lady Godiva* and O'Keefe's *Peeping Tom*, and as Miss la Blonde in *The Romp*. Acting alongside her in *The Romp* was one Mrs Jordan, the long-term mistress of the Duke of Clarence. While Mrs Jordan died destitute in France, Harriot went on to become the mistress, then wife, of the ageing banker Thomas Coutts, and later Duchess of St Albans.

Emma Hamilton

From the viewpoint of the twenty-first century, it would be easy to imagine that Lady Hamilton was the most famous mistress of the Georgian age. However, after her death in obscurity in 1815, her existence was covered up for nearly a century.

Born Amy or Emma Lyon, she lost her virginity when one of her male relatives was press-ganged. She applied to his captain, John Willet Payne, for his freedom. He granted it for a price – her own body. She posed nude as an example of perfect health and beauty in Dr James Graham's Temple of Health and worked as a nude model for Thomas Gainsborough, Joshua Reynolds and other artists. She may have been a prostitute too. Later she was taken up by Sir Harry Featherstonehaugh, who moved her into a cottage on his estate at Uppark in Sussex, where she danced naked on the dining room table.

When Featherstonehaugh tired of her, she moved in with a friend of his named Charles Grenville, who showed her off at the Ranelagh pleasure gardens. But Grenville was short of money and, when his childless uncle, the British ambassador to Naples, Sir William Hamilton, took a shine to her, he suggested that Sir William take Emma under his protection in return for making Grenville his heir.

Emma headed off to Naples, where she became the learned Hamilton's mistress. In his *Travels in Italy*, Goethe wrote that Hamilton had reached an age where he found, 'after his long study of art and nature, the summit of all joy in nature and art in a beautiful young girl'. Though 40 years her senior, he was a vigorous old roué who paid to watch youths of both sexes swimming in the sea.

Emma became famous in Neapolitan society for her 'attitudes' – she would adopt the classical poses found on the antique Greek vases Sir William collected. Although it is said that she wore classical Greek dress for this, at least one engraving shows her naked. There was also a rumour that she had an affair with the promiscuous Queen Caroline of Naples in her famously debauched court. In September 1791, while visiting London, she married Hamilton, signing the register in Marylebone parish church as 'Amy Lyon'.

Nelson first set eyes on Lady Hamilton in Naples in September 1793 and was immediately smitten. When he returned to Naples in 1798 after the Battle of the Nile, he was greeted as a national hero, because his victory in Egypt had saved the Kingdom of the Two Sicilies – Naples and Sicily itself – from invasion by the French. It was then they became very intimate.

Nelson travelled back to England overland with Emma and her husband, though it was clear that they were lovers. Nelson moved out from his wife and lived in a *ménage à trois* with the Hamiltons at 23 Piccadilly in London. This caused an enormous scandal and the three were ostracised by the court. Emma then fell pregnant by Nelson and gave birth to their daughter Horatia.

Hamilton tolerated being mocked as a cuckold until just before his death, when he complained that 'the whole of the attention of my wife is given to Lord N'. Before Nelson left for Trafalgar, he and Emma took communion in the local parish church and exchanged rings in what he considered to be a marriage in the eyes of God.

After Nelson's death Emma's extravagance mired her in debt and in 1813 she found herself in the King's Bench debtors' prison in Southwark. With money from Nelson's brother, she left prison and took her daughter Horatia to live in Calais, where she drank herself to death. There is a memorial to her in the Parc Richelieu in the centre of Calais.

Horatia was taken in by Nelson's sister and later married. She acknowledged that Nelson was her father but, until her death, denied that Emma was her mother. This allowed Victorian historians to make out that, at most, Lady Hamilton had had a platonic relationship with Nelson. It became a sex secret until the centenary of Trafalgar and the publication of Walter Sichel's *Emma, Lady Hamilton* in 1905.

Posture girls

Emma Hamilton's practice of posing nude was very much in vogue in Georgian times. *The History of the Human Heart, or the Adventures of a Young Gentleman*, published in London in 1769, talked of 'posture girls who stripped stark naked and mounted themselves upon the middle of the table'. And in *A Rake's Progress* Hogarth shows a young woman undressing, ready to be served up nude on a silver salver.

The *New Atalantis* of 1762, mentioned 'Posture Nan, the greatest mistress in that way of any of her sex'. And, according to *Midnight Spy* of 1766, there was a house in Russell Street where there was 'an object that at once excites our aversion and pity – a fine woman extended on the floor, exposing those parts, which, was she not thus deprived of all sense, she would labour on such occasions to conceal. Being addicted to drams, she generally comes into this house much elevated, and having drunk three or four gills of Madeira, frequently exhibits to the company this shocking spectacle. So she is carried out like a beast; and the savages deride her condition, and are delighted with such a prostitution of matchless beauty.'

Nineteenth-century gentlemen preferred more refined titillation. They went to the *poses plastiques*, where naked young women adopted poses from classical art and literature. This was considered very uplifting.

Foul mouths

In the eighteenth century, foreign visitors were shocked at the foul mouths of upper-class English women.

'Good round oaths are often heard from the lips of gentle-women, who are quite familiar with the slang of the sportsman and the stable,' wrote Ivan Bloch. In his book *Sexual Life in England*, he related a tale to back his case.

One day the Duchess of Marlborough called on the Chief Justice Lord Mansfield, omitting to give her name to the manservant who answered the door. When Mansfield asked who was calling, the hapless servant said, 'I couldn't find out who she was, my Lord, but she swore so stiff that she must be a lady of quality.'

The satirist Jonathan Swift also remarked upon the sexual content of women's conversation, saying:

Or how should I, alas, relate
The sum off all their senseless prate,
Their innuendoes, hints and slanders
Their meanings lewd and double entanders!
Now comes the general scandal charge,
What some invent, the rest enlarge.

Blue stockings

The rise of the Puritan and the ribaldry of the Restoration set back the cause of women. In the eighteenth century, women's-only debating societies were set up, but these seem to have failed to inspire sisterly solidarity, partly because of the number of young men who got in dressed as women.

By then, women's reading matter had turned positively pornographic. In a scene in Sheridan's *The Rivals* (1775), Lydia Languish is settling down with some juicy books brought by her maid Lucy, when she is surprised.

LYDIA: Wait. Somebody's coming. Quick. See who it is.

LUCY: Oh! It's my Lord and your Aunt.

LYDIA: Quick. Lucy, dear. Hide the books. Throw *Tanzai* under my toilet. Put *Adultère Innocent* behind *Human Duties*. Push Ovid under the pillow, and *Bijoux Indiscrets* into your pocket.

And in *The Hermit of London*, published in Paris in 1820, French travel writer Victor Joseph Étienne de Jouy relates how he found an extremely erotic novel left behind by two ladies in Kensington Gardens.

Masked balls

The masques of the seventeenth century developed into the elaborate masked balls of the eighteenth. With people's faces covered and their identity disguised by lavish costumes, these balls presented the perfect opportunity for all sorts of amorous adventures. Naturally, a number of 'Cyprians' – devotees of Venus, the goddess of Cyprus – took advantage of the anonymity to ply their trade. In 1726, the Bishop of London condemned fancy-dress balls from the pulpit of Bow Church, and in 1729 the Grand Jury of Middlesex denounced them as the 'principal promoters of vice and immorality'.

Of course, the idea of what constituted fancy dress was open to wide interpretation. Lady Elizabeth Montagu, attending one in 1750, noted,

> Miss Chudleigh's dress, or rather undress, was remarkable. She represented Iphigenia [the daughter of Agamemnon] before her sacrifice; but so naked the high priest might easily examine the entrails of the victim. The maids of honour (not, of maids, the strictest) were so offended, they would not speak to her.

Rakes and libertines

The eighteenth-century rake was immortalised by the artist William Hogarth in *A Rake's Progress*, a series of eight paintings and engravings. The originals now hang in the Sir John Soane Museum in Lincoln's Inn Fields. A rake was defined as an unmarried young man with an annual income of £2,000, around £200,000 today. Ninety per cent of that would be spent on amusement – first and last, the pursuit of women.

'The real rake gambles, drinks, fucks, talks of amorous pills and bougies as we would speak of candied fruits or sweets,' said eighteenth-century German writer Georg Christoph Lichtenberg. 'He turns night into day and day into night … ruins the innocent creatures who love him, fights duels with persons whose honour he has injured, spends money extravagantly, his own and that of other people, and all this is for the purpose of acquiring a reputation for himself.'

The rake would rise at noon or even three in the afternoon. He would take breakfast, then go for a ride or a walk. At eight, he would dine with friends, talking until eleven. Then they would go to the Vauxhall Gardens and spend another £20 – £2,000 at today's prices – on bad wine. He would then visit a brothel or two. This was the fashionable thing to do. And he would get home at four in the morning.

The fun-loving guys were called rakes by those who condemned them, as rake was short for rakehell or rackhell – where they would surely end up. They would have called themselves libertines, which had political overtones. It derived from the Latin for a freed slave and denoted a religious free-thinker and political radical, as well a debauchee.

The English Don Juan

Foreign observers were amazed how cool, calm and collected English libertines were. French and Italian Don Juans, it seems, were driven from conquest to conquest by passion. Even Teutonic rakes seethed with emotion. But the English Don Juan 'seduces on principle for the sake of experiment; he pursues love as a kind of sport', wrote Georg Christoph Lichtenberg.

Lord Queensbury gave air to this sang-froid in a letter to George Selwyn in 1766. It read, 'Bully [Viscount Bolingbroke] is appearing again in society, and swears that he will seduce any innocent girl whatever. I do not doubt that he will.'

Literary critic Hippolyte-Adolphe Taine pointed out that the English womaniser depicted by Samuel Richardson in his novel *Clarissa* was very different from the type depicted by Mozart or Molière.

'Unyielding in pride,' he wrote, 'the desire to subjugate others, the provocative love of battle, the need for ascendancy, these are his predominant features. Sensuality is but of secondary importance compared to these. He will spare an innocent girl because he knows the conquest would be too easy and because her grandmother begs him not to seduce her. His motto is: humiliate the proud ...'

Midnight Spy in 1766 related the tale of the son of an eminent apothecary in Red Lion Square named Bamwell, who was 'the reigning debauchee of his time and so great a favourite with the women that he frequently boasts that no girl can resist him'. He systematically seduced numerous young girls and, having 'formed an unhappy girl perfectly for vice, to render her totally callous, he introduces her to the company of his abandoned acquaintance, by which means he comes off without paying his reckoning'.

Old Q

The greatest libertine of the age was William Douglas, the second Earl of March and the fourth Duke of Queensberry. His status is confirmed by the latest edition of the *Dictionary of National Biography*, which describes him as a 'sybarite and politician'. It says that, after he came of age and moved to London, he 'dedicated himself to the pursuit of pleasure' and was 'universally admired by the ladies'. He also financed the Italian opera in London, taking the leading divas Anna Zamparini and Teresina Tondino as his mistresses.

'Indeed it was as a pursuer and seducer of the opposite sex that March would be most remembered,' continues the *DNB*. 'He had a long string of mistresses, whom he neither flaunted nor concealed.' But he died unmarried. He had at least one child, a daughter by the Marchesa Fagnani, who was brought up by his friend – and fellow rake – George Selwyn and went on to marry the marquess of Hertford.

In his house opposite Green Park, Queensberry, dressed as a shepherd, once re-enacted the judgement of Paris with three of the most beautiful women in London, awarding the winner a golden apple. He also numbered among his mistresses the daughter of the prime minister Henry Pelham. When her father prohibited the liaison, she took to playing faro and dissipated her entire fortune.

Well into old age, Douglas continued to pursue young women and earned the humorous epithet 'Old Q'.

At the age of 86 he could still be seen sitting in the porch or leering from the windows of his house at 138 Piccadilly at beautiful young women passing below. His deathbed was covered with more than 70 love letters from 'females of every description and of every rank from duchesses down to ladies of the easiest virtue'.

After Old Q died, his house in Piccadilly was divided into two. Half of it was occupied by Lord Byron, who shocked even decadent Georgian society with his adulterous affair with Lady Caroline Lamb, his bisexuality, his rumoured preference for anal sex, his incestuous affair with his half-sister and his shameless promiscuity on the Continent.

Paradise lost

There was extraordinarily high rate of suicide among English libertines. Often they killed themselves in brothels. One such was John Damer the son of Lord Milton. On 15 August 1776, he went to one of the capital's most fashionable brothels and hired 12 of the prettiest girls and a blind fiddler. He entertained them with a sumptuous meal. Then the doors were closed. He got the girls to strip off, then had them dance for him naked and 'entertain him with voluptuous poses' for several hours. Then he paid them a guinea each – £100 today – and shot himself. He was just 32.

Blind fiddlers

Blind fiddlers were much in demand in the eighteenth century. When Giacomo Casanova was in London, he and Welbore Ellis Agar, son of Henry Agar MP and grandson of the Bishop of Meath, were in the Cannon coffeehouse in Cockspur Street, where they met a pretty young woman, who had a friend. Agar suggested they have a '*partie carrée*' – the unmarried version of a wife-swapping party. The two girls, Casanova said, were 'truly created for joy' and Agar called for a blind fiddler so they could dance the hornpipe 'in the costume of Adam and Eve'. Agar later rose to become Commissioner of Customs.

The Cock and Hen Club

The Cock and Hen Club was founded in March 1788. 'Under this title, licentious creatures gathered in the parish of Clerkenwell,' said a visitor to London. 'The club had a male and female president. Here unbridled excesses were carried on, disturbing the neighbours.'

They called the authorities and 15 constables raided the club. They found 157 people of both sexes, most hopelessly drunk. The members defended themselves with sticks and shovels, but were eventually overpowered. Many escaped by jumping out of the windows or off the roof. But 60 were captured and taken to prison.

The Hell-Fire Club

The most famous of the eighteenth-century blasphemous societies was the Hell-Fire Club. It was founded by Sir Francis Dashwood in 1721, when he was still in his teens. Although he remained a committed Christian throughout his life, Dashwood claimed to have used the black mass to raise the Devil. Despite being condemned by George I, Dashwood continued his sacrilegious activities.

In 1728, Dashwood attempted to 'fornicate his way across Europe'. He visited Rome and attended the ceremonial scourging of Christ in the Sistine Chapel on Good Friday. During the ceremony, Dashwood pulled a real whip from under his coat, cried '*Il Diavolo*' and viciously lashed the congregation. He was ejected and, later, expelled from Italy for the outrage. Back in England he continued his debauchery.

Dashwood's Hell-Fire Club was by no means the only satanic organisation in eighteenth-century England. Young bucks amused themselves at the Banditti, the Blasters and the Sons of Midnight. These clubs emulated the French obsession with debauchery linked with Devil worship. There were at least three Hell-Fire Clubs in London and three more in Scotland. They offered unlimited access to alcohol, drugs and free sex.

However, Dashwood's club was undoubtedly the most exclusive. Membership boasted Frederick, Prince of Wales, the Earl of Bute – who became prime minister – the Earl of Sandwich, Member of Parliament John Wilkes and novelist Lawrence Sterne.

Meetings were held in The George and Vulture in George Yard, London. There a naked girl spread-eagled on the bar-room table was used as an altar. A communion wafer was pushed up her vagina and the sacrificial wine was drunk from her navel and, when the Black Mass was over, there was an orgy.

When Dashwood married in 1745, his Hell-Fire Club ceased its activities. But in 1753, it resumed again at Med-menham Abbey, near West Wycombe in Buckinghamshire. A complete satanic temple was excavated in the chalk caves there. members were now called 'monks' and wore red habits. The caves were hung with inverted crosses and various idols. One resembled a bird with its head turned around so that its phallus-shaped beak protruded from its back. Women would ride this this to ready themselves for the mass orgies that would follow. Monks also had individual cells where they could per-form private rituals. Prostitutes dressed as nuns were shipped in from London for rites and orgies. Some local girls looking for excitement also joined in, as did a number of society ladies. They would arrive masked and review the monks, only remov-ing their masks when they were sure there was no one there who would recognise them and tell their husbands.

CHAPTER THIRTEEN

Victoriana

T IS EASY TO THINK of the Victorian era as very strait-laced. The woman on the throne wore widow's weeds for 40 years. However, she came from a promiscuous family. Her widowed mother took a lover. Victoria herself proposed to Prince Albert, after being overawed by his beauty, though he was something of a disappointment in bed. Their bedroom at Osborne was soon hung with paintings of male nudes in the hope of stimulating her reluctant lover. She hated being pregnant, as it gave Albert an excuse to abstain from sex for up to a year.

When Albert died, it is clear that she had an affair with her gillie John Brown. After he died, she became close to her Indian secretary Abdul Karim and would not listen to those who said that that it was inappropriate for her to be intimate with a 'black man' – a term she abhorred.

The Prince of Wales

Through most of Victoria's reign, her son, Bertie, Prince of Wales, continued the family tradition for wayward behaviour, seducing actresses, including Lillie Langtry, spending his time in the brothels of Paris, and narrowly escaping appearances in the divorce courts.

In one case, the defendant, Lady Mordaunt, was declared insane so that divorce proceedings naming him as co-respondent could not go ahead. When Bertie became Edward VII in 1901, at the coronation a balcony above the chancel in Westminster Abbey was reserved for his mistresses. It was referred to as 'the King's loose-box'.

To mend a broken heart

According to Henry Theophilus Finck, by Victorian times, every nation had developed its own local remedy for a broken heart: 'The Spaniards by stabbing the girl who broke it; the Italians by annihilating the rival; the Germans by soaking the fragments in Rhine wine; the Englishmen by a change of air.'

But, in the end, 'they all follow the example of the Frenchman who, on the day following the catastrophe, casts his eyes about for a new charmer; or, if they do not, but like a snail withdraw into their shells for the rest of their life, abusing all women as heartless, they are bigger fools than they look. What would you say of a fisherman who went out for a day's sport and returned after an hour because the first trout that nibbled at the bait escaped?'

Victorian vixens

In 1860, it was estimated that there were 80,000 prostitutes in London alone. Despite their high mortality, their numbers kept increasing. Some of them became fêted beauties who were courted by gentlemen of wealth and position. These included Polly Ash, 'Sweet Nellie' Fowler – so-called because of her natural body scent – and Laura Bell, who became an evangelical preacher when she retired from her youthful calling. Queen of the courtesans was 'Skittles', who hailed from Liverpool. The young Earl of Hartington – the future Duke of Devonshire – begged her to marry him, but she enjoyed her promiscuous ways too much. She had won her nickname, it was said, when she knocked down a group of drunken Guards officers 'like a row of skittles'.

English women also made their mark among the *grandes horizontales* of Paris. One of the most famous Parisian courtesans of the Second Empire was Cora Pearl, who hailed from Plymouth. Famously, she had herself served up at dinner on a silver salver, completely naked except for a string of pearls and a sprig of parsley, and she charged Emperor Napoleon III £10,000 for a single night.

Victorian brothels

In his survey of prostitution of 1838, James Beard Talbot also found that there were 355 brothels in Dublin, 219 in Edinburgh, 770 in Liverpool, 308 in Manchester, 797 in Birmingham, 204 in Glasgow, 175 in Hull, 175 in Leeds and 194 in Norwich. In London he counted 5,000, while there were only 2,150 schools, churches and charitable institutions. Some brothels hid behind charitable names. One called itself the Institution for the Care of Children, where numerous young women prostituted themselves each night.

White slave trade

During the Victorian era, old England was the centre of an international trade in prostitutes. According to the *Pall Mall Gazette* of 10 July 1885, London was 'the greatest market of human flesh in the whole world', consisting of both 'imports and exports'. It went on to talk of a 'ghastly' chapter concerning the import of foreign girls into England. 'The difference between the two is that in England vice is free, whereas on the Continent it is a legalised slavery, and that of course is immense,' said the paper, adding, 'Girls are regularly brought over to London from France, Belgium, Germany, and Switzerland for the purpose of being ruined.'

In a letter dated 3 April 1878, an Irish woman using the pseudonym Raphael, who worked for the trafficker John Sellecarts, offered a Belgian buyer 'two lovely English girls who wish to go into a "House" ', which she would deliver to Ostend. The price was 300 francs for each girl and she stressed that 'their true age and all papers are quite in order'. This was a regular order.

Another trafficker told the *Pall Mall Gazette* that he was exporting around 250 girls a year, a third of whom were already prostitutes. The other two-thirds discovered their fate only when they were locked up in a foreign brothel. One brothel in Brussels was stocked almost exclusively with English girls between the ages of 12 and 14.

The import traffic was principally in virgins when the demand for maidens reached its peak in the nineteenth century.

Saving fallen women

The great parliamentarian William Ewart Gladstone, a loving husband and father of eight, felt empathy for fallen women. When he was prime minister, he would pick up girls in the street and take them back to 10 Downing Street, though other members of the Cabinet begged him not to.

Apologists point out that Gladstone was a fierce moralist and a lay preacher, and contended that all he did with his 'erring sisters' behind closed doors was read them an uplifting passage from the Bible. Indeed, he did manage to guide some of the young women he brought home into honest employment.

However, in his own diaries Gladstone admitted that his motives were partly, at least, 'carnal'. He had visited prostitutes when he was a young man at Oxford in the 1820s. This left him tormented by guilt and he would scourge himself afterwards. He married in 1839, but in 1843, after he joined Robert Peel's government as president of the Board of Trade, he wrote in his diary that he was 'fearful [of] the guilt of sin returning again and again in forms ever new but alike hideous'.

Although he tried to channel his urges through pornography, he still visited a prostitute named Elizabeth Collins – sometimes as often as every other day. Afterwards, he always scourged himself. This continued after he became Chancellor of the Exchequer in 1852. Once, he was blackmailed by someone who saw him pick up a prostitute, but he handed the blackmailer to the police.

As prime minister, Gladstone had a close friendship with the Prince of Wales's mistress, the actress Lillie Langtry. And in the 1870s there were rumours that he was having an affair with Madame Olga Novikov, who advised him on Russian affairs.

But he could not give up prostitutes. In 1880, when he was 70, he was still visiting brothels on what he called 'rescue work', in spite of warnings that his activities might be discovered by the press.

Perhaps he did nothing but watch. Some of the girls called him 'Glad-eyes'; others 'Daddy-do-nothing'. Gladstone was 82 when he gave up seeing prostitutes. His reputation, however, remained. When he died at the age of 88, one obituary read, 'Gladstone founded the great tradition, in public to speak the language of the highest and strictest principle, and in private to pursue and possess every sort of woman.'

He was a true Victorian.

Disraeli

Gladstone's great political rival was Benjamin Disraeli who is reputed to have said to Gladstone, 'When you are out saving fallen women, save one for me.'

Disraeli too had had his fair share of scandal. After a youthful tour of the Middle East, he became noticeably effeminate, dressing in green velvet trousers and ruffles. He spoke openly at dinner parties of his passion for the East and, according to the painter Benjamin Haydon, 'seemed tinged with a disposition to palliate its infamous vices ... sodomy'.

Disraeli's biographer Jane Ridley concurred. 'Bisexuality came as naturally to Disraeli as did Tory Radicalism,' she said.

Back in England he had a series of affairs with older women, some of whom were married. His affair with Henrietta Sykes became a public scandal. She was much older than he and had been married for 11 years to the ailing Sir Francis Sykes, who was the father of her four children. Her letters to Disraeli were signed 'your mother'.

Despite the gossip, they were seen out together at parties and the opera. Her husband turned a blind eye because he was having an affair with Clara Bolton at the time. Clara was another of Disraeli's former lovers. She was jealous and encouraged Sir Francis to break up the affair. He did, but soon afterwards he found his wife in bed with yet another man. In a fit of pique, he kicked her out of the house and placed a notice in the newspapers advertising her adultery, causing a scandal that tainted everyone involved, including Disraeli.

His election as MP for Maidstone at a fifth attempt resulted in accusations of bribery and a court case. His costs were paid by the latest woman in his life, Mary Anne Wyndham Lewis, the widow of his late rival for the Maidstone seat. She was 12 years older than Disraeli and rich. They married.

While Disraeli continued making his way to the top of the greasy pole, the Conservative Party was kept out of power by another sex scandal. At the age of 79, the Liberal leader Lord Palmerston – a well-known womaniser nicknamed 'Lord Cupid' – was cited as co-respondent in the divorce case of the attractive 30-year-old Mrs O'Kane. She claimed to have committed adultery with him in the Houses of Parliament, leading to the inevitable joke 'she was Kane and he was able'. Disraeli said that it was shame that this got out, as Palmerston would sweep the country. He did. At the next election, the Liberals won by a landslide.

Later, Disraeli tried to emulate his political rival. After his wife died in 1872, he began romantic liaisons with two sisters, Lady Bradford and Lady Chesterfield, which he maintained until his death in 1881.

CHAPTER FOURTEEN

Pederasty

ESPITE THE PROPENSITIES of various monarchs, there was no such thing as homosexuality in old England. The word did not come into the English language till 1892 with C.G. Chaddock's translation of Richard von Krafft-Ebing's *Psychopathia Sexualis*, which maintained the 'condition' was an aberration. Before that, men who preferred men had been condemned as sodomites, buggers or pederasts.

Oscar Wilde and his coterie described themselves as Uranists, which was something of a new coinage.

Sodomy

During the reign of Richard I – widely thought to have indulged himself – those convicted of sodomy were hanged, burned, stoned to death, buried alive or drowned. Henry VIII passed a Buggery Act and his son Edward VI passed a Sodomy Act for good measure. Then in 1562 Elizabeth I again banned the 'detestable vice of buggery' after her sister Mary had

legalised it in the first year of her reign 'to the high displeasure of Almighty God'.

James I of England, though indulging himself, condemned two men accused of sodomy to be burned at the stake in Edinburgh in 1570. He also burned witches in Scotland, but when he came to England in 1603 he mellowed. Indeed, during the 45 years of Elizabeth I's reign and the 23 years of James's in England, only six men in the Home Counties were indicted of sodomy – and only one convicted – even though a contemporary diarist recorded in London in 1622 that the 'sinne of sodomye' was widespread 'in this wicked cittye'.

During the English Civil War, a number of priests declared that Parliament had no authority over them, so they could do what they liked. Parliament struck back, sequestering their offices.

Among the 'scandalous and malignant priests' denounced by Parliament on 14 November 1643 was John Wilson, vicar of Arlington, Sussex. He was condemned for attempting to commit buggery with three of his male parishioners rather than have sex with women, 'to avoid the shame and danger that oft ensueth in begetting bastards'.

It was also alleged that he had buggered 18 men, attempted to commit buggery with a mare, baptised a bastard child – declaring openly in church 'that our Saviour as he was in the flesh was a bastard' – and 'hath openly affirmed that buggery is no sinne'. And he was accused of frequenting ale houses and being a 'great drinker'. He was, of course, a royalist.

The Mollies' Club

When the court of Charles II returned from the Continent in 1660, it brought with it a certain tolerance of homosexuality learned abroad. The Earl of Rochester even wrote an outrageous play called *Sodom*. But, given his scandalous interest in women, little notice was taken.

Then in the eighteenth century the authorities began to crack down. In his *History of London Clubs* (1709), Edward Ward wrote,

There is a particular gang of sodomitical wretches in this town, who call themselves the Mollies, and are so far degenerated from all masculine deportment, or manly exercise, that they rather fancy themselves women, imitating all the little vanities that custom has reconciled to the female sex, affecting to speak, walk, tattle, curtsy, cry, scold, and to mimick all manner of effeminacy that ever has fallen within their several observations; not omitting the indecencies of lewd women ... .

Then there was the joy of motherhood. Ward wrote of how they 'cushioned up the belly' of one of their number, dressing him in women's clothes and getting him to mimic 'a groaning woman' at the point of childbirth, the 'wooden off-spring to be afterwards Christened'. One thing led to another.

> No sooner had they ended their feast and run thro' all the ceremonies of gossiping, but, having washed away with wine all fear of shame, they began to enter upon their beastly obscenities and to take those infamous liberties with one another, that no man who is not sunk into the state of devilism can think on without blushing, or mention without a Christian abhorrence of all such heathenish brutalities.

All this went on behind closed doors. Even so retribution was sure to follow.

> Thus, without detection, they continued their odious society for some years, till their sodomitical practices were happily discovered by the cunning management of some of the under-agents to the Reforming Society; so several were brought to open shame and punishment; others flying from justice to escape the ignominy, that by this means the diabolical society were forced to put a period to their filthy scandalous revels.

Pretty fellows

In 1749, *Satan's Harvest Home* warned about the 'effeminacy of men's dress and manners, particularly their kissing each other'. The ornate men's fashions of the eighteenth century – powdered wigs and luxurious fabrics – encouraged sodomy, the author maintained.

'I am content no age can produce anything so preposterous as the present dress of those gentlemen who called themselves pretty fellows: their head-dress especially, which wants nothing but a suit of pinners [a woman's cap with flaps at the side] to make them downright women.'

Not only were these fashions effeminate, they also made it 'difficult to know a gentleman from a footman'.

> The low-heeled pump is an emblem of their low spirits; the great harness buckle is the height of affectation; the silk waistcoat all belaced, with a scurvy blue coat like a livery frock, has something so poorly preposterous, it quite enrages me ... But what renders all more intolerable is the hair stroked over before and cocked up behind with a comb sticking in it, as if it were just ready to receive a head-dress.

Kissing

Then there was the habit of men's kissing openly in the streets.

'But of all the customs effeminacy has produced, none more hateful, predominant, and pernicious, than that of men kissing each other,' said the author of *Satan's Harvest Home*. 'This fashion was brought over from Italy (the mother and nurse of sodomy); where the master is oftener intriguing with the page than a fair lady …'

This led to other perceived iniquities, this time in France, where the ladies 'in the nunneries' were 'criminally amorous of each other'.

I am shocked to the last degree; but not so much as when I see two fulsome fellows slavering every time they meet … And tho' many gentlemen of worth are oftentimes, out of pure good manners, obliged to give into it; yet the land will never be purged of its abominations till this unmanly, unnatural usage be totally abolished: For it is the first inlet to the detestable sin of sodomy.

And he got his way. Towards the end of the eighteenth century, men stopped kissing in public in England. A German visitor warned, 'No embrace is admitted between men, and laughter would be aroused by doing so, as a bow and hand-shaking are the only forms of civility recognised.'

While kissing continued on the Continent, it lost favour in England as the 'kiss of friendship between men is strictly avoided as inclining towards the sin regarded in England as more abominable than any other'.

However, women continued to kiss into the nineteenth century.

Clare Market

Clare Market was the foremost centre of sodomy in London. In 1794, policemen from Bow Street had raided the Bunch of Grapes there.

'On entering the room, the guard found two fellows in women's attire, with muffs and wide shawls and most fashionable turban-like bonnets, silken pinafores, etc.,' said one report. 'Their faces were painted and powdered, and they were dancing a minuet in the middle of the room, while the others were standing around watching them in improper attitudes.'

Eighteen were arrested and, still in women's dresses, taken before the magistrate to be questioned. 'It turned out that each member of the club had a woman's name, such as "Lady Golding", "Countess Papillon", "Miss Fanny", etc., by which he was known to other members of this shameful company,' said the report, adding that crowds outside threw stones at the men and threatened to lynch them as they were led from the court to prison.

Other Molly houses

There were numerous Molly houses throughout the metropolis. According to *The Phoenix of Sodom, or the Vere Street Coterie, Being an Exhibition of the Gambols Practised by the Ancient Lechers of Sodom and Gomorrah*, lawyer Robert Holloway's 1813 account of the goings-on at the White Swan, 'It seems that these odious practices are not confined to one, two, or three houses, either public or private; for there are many about town: one in the vicinity of the Strand; one near the Obelisk, St George's-fields.'

And the practice was not restricted to London. Holloway reported that 25 years earlier there was

a society of the same order with the Vere-street gang, in the City of Exeter, most of whom were men of rank and local situation; they were apprehended, and about fifteen of them tried; and, though they were acquitted by the letter of the law, the enraged multitude was so convinced of their guilt, that, without any respect to their rank, they burnt them in effigy.

Helping hand

The tourist guide called the *Yokel's Perceptor; or more sprees in London etc.*, published in the 1850s, pointed out where those who were interested could find 'Margeries, Pooffs, and Mary Anns ...

The Quadrant, Holborn, Fleet Street and the Strand are full of them. Not so very long ago signs and bills were hung in the windows of respectable hotels in the vicinity of Charing Cross with the notice: 'Beware of paederasts!' They usually gather near the picture shops, and are recognisable by their effeminate appearance, fashionable clothing, etc.

They had little difficulty finding wealthy customers, since there was a great deal of homosexuality around in the upper classes. Its expression was fostered by public schools and all-male colleges at Oxford and Cambridge. The campaigning editor of the *Pall Mall Gazette*, W.T. Stead, wrote at the time of the trial of Oscar Wilde,

> Should everyone found guilty of Oscar Wilde's crime be imprisoned, there would be a very surprising emigration from Eton, Harrow, Rugby and Winchester to the jails of Pentonville and Holloway. Until then, boys are free to pick up tendencies and habits in public schools for which they may be sentenced to hard labour later on.

Cleveland Street

In 1886, the police raided a homosexual brothel at 19 Cleveland Street. When the owners were arrested, they dropped the names of their aristocratic clients. These included the then Prince of Wales's son, Eddy, and the superintendent of his stables, Lord Arthur Somerset, along with the Earl of Euston.

The names of these high-born gentlemen were kept out of the subsequent trial, which earned the low-born brothel keepers nine months' hard labour. However, Ernest Parke, the crusading editor of the *North London Press*, published the names of Somerset and Euston.

Somerset fled to France, where he stayed until his death in 1926, but Euston sued for libel. He claimed that he had been given a flier advertising '*poses plastiques*' – which employed nude girls posing in classical Greek attitudes – at 19 Cleveland

Street. Naturally, when he went there he had discovered what was really going on, and was appalled and fled.

But that was not what John Saul, one of the boys who worked at the brothel, said. He said that Lord Euston had picked him up on the street and had taken him back to Cleveland Street for sex. But Euston was 'not an actual sodomite', Saul said. 'He likes to play with you and then "spend" on your belly.'

The judge dismissed Saul as a 'loathsome object'. Parke went down for a year with hard labour. Lord Euston was appointed Edward VII's aide-de-camp at his coronation in 1901. Eddy had died at Sandringham in 1892, probably of syphilis.

Oscar Wilde

The trial of Oscar Wilde, a married man with two young sons, was one of the great sex scandals of the Victorian era. It is widely assumed that he was prosecuted because he had a homosexual affair with Lord Alfred Douglas, known affectionately as 'Bosie'.

True, they had been lovers when Wilde first met the 20-year-old Bosie in 1891. But both men had a taste for younger flesh and the evidence presented at Wilde's trial in 1895 showed that they shared lovers, often underaged boys, who were paid off or coerced into silence. They took adjoining suites in the Savoy and passed catamites between them with disastrous consequences for the bed linen, as the chambermaids later testified.

The 'love that dare not speak its name' was not a line of

Wilde's, but comes from a poem called 'Two Loves' by Bosie. And it refers not to homosexual love but to the Socratic ideal of the love between an older man and a youth.

Bosie and Wilde called themselves Uranists, which comes from a reference made by Plato in his Symposiums to the Greek goddess of love Aphrodite – also known as Urania. They saw themselves as part of a political movement calling for the 'new Hellenism', which sought the legalisation of what we would now consider paedophilia. The vanguard for this movement was called the Order of Chaeronea, after the battle where the Theban Band of gay warriors were slaughtered in 338 BC. Wilde was an early recruit.

In 1895, Wilde fell foul of the Protection of Women and Suppression of Brothels Act 1885 (though no women or girls were involved). Although sodomy had long been against the law, it was extraordinarily difficult to secure a conviction, since the prosecution had to prove the actual 'emission of seed' in the rectum. However, thanks to evidence collected by W.T. Stead, editor of the *Pall Mall Gazette*, it was clear at the time that there was widespread male prostitution in English cities and maverick Liberal MP Henry Labouchère managed to add an amendment to the Protection of Women Bill, which provided for any male procuring or trying to procure an act of gross indecency with another male to go to prison for a maximum of two years, with or without hard labour.

The prosecution against Wilde went ahead only because Bosie's father, the Marquis of Queensberry, threatened to reveal that leading members of the Liberal government were homosexuals. These included the prime minister Lord Rosebery, who had had an affair with Bosie's older brother and

Queensberry's eldest son, Viscount Drumlanrig. Fearing exposure Drumlanrig, a junior minister in Rosebery's government, had shot himself.

Wilde was found guilty on seven counts of gross indecency and sentenced to two years with hard labour, the maximum permitted. It has to be said, he got off lightly. Today Wilde would be considered a paedophile and would receive a much longer sentence, as well as being put on the Sex Offenders Register.

Nor did he suffer terribly in jail. Sympathetic members of the Liberal government organised soft treatment for him. After a year, Wilde recanted. He no longer posed as a Uranian martyr and petitioned the home secretary for his release on the grounds that he was suffering from 'sexual madness', saying that his lust for young men was a 'strange disease'. When that failed, he began – with the collusion of the warder – having sex with other inmates. Nor did he learn his lesson. After he was released, Wilde travelled around the Continent, seducing young men wherever he went. He died in Paris in 1900.

CHAPTER FIFTEEN

Sapphism

IKE 'homosexual', 'lesbian' in the modern sense was a new coinage from the 1890s. Until then, Lesbian meant an inhabitant of the Greek island of Lesbos or the sweet wine produced there. The term came into usage because the poet and teacher Sappho, who lived on the island in the sixth century BCE, wrote paeans to the young girls in her care. Until the end of the nineteenth century, women who preferred their own gender were called tribades.

Literary lesbians

The first mention of tribadism in English literature seems to be in Sir Philip Sidney's *Arcadia*, written in 1598. In one passage, two princesses go to bed together.

> They adorned the bed with their prettiest clothes, so that on this night it surpassed the couch of Venus. Then they caressed each other, exchanging tender, though chaste,

embraces and sweet, though cold, kisses. It seemed as though the God of Love were playing with them without his arrow, or that, tired of his own fervour, had come to refresh himself between their sweet lips.

Gender benders

There were some notable cross-dressers in old England. One was Mary Firth, alias Mary Markham, who became a highwaywoman under the name Moll Cutpurse. 'Cutpurse' meant a pickpocket, but in this context it is also a risqué pun, 'purse' being slang for scrotum and 'cut' being a crude reference to the vulva. Born in the 1580s in Aldersgate Street, London, she became a pimp, providing young women for men and lovers for middle-class wives.

During the Civil War, she robbed the parliamentary commander-in-chief General Fairfax, wounding him in the arm and shooting the horses of two of his servants in the process. She escaped the gallows by handing over a vast bribe of £2,000 – the equivalent of over £200,000 today. Under the Commonwealth she made money by perfecting the art of forging Oliver Cromwell's signature. She amassed £5,000, but when she died in Fleet Street in 1659 only £100 remained, which she distributed among friends and servants. She asked to be buried face down. The marble stone that covered her grave was destroyed in the Great Fire of London of 1666.

Another highwaywoman in men's clothes was discovered when she tried to rob the notorious highwayman Thomas Rumbold, who was hanged in 1689. The ensuing fight ended when Rumbold bound his opponent hand and foot. Then he began to search his adversary, undid 'his' coat and discovered that 'he' was a she.

At 15, she had married an innkeeper and, as a barmaid, discovered which patrons were carrying money, then, dressed as a man, stopped them on the road and robbed them. She even robbed her own husband.

Pirates

Not all pirates were men. Irish-born Anne Cormac was raised in South Carolina, eventually falling for a ne'er-do-well called James Bonny, who took her to New Providence Island in the Bahamas, where reformed pirates were allowed to settle. There, James Bonny turned informer and Anne Bonny met the swaggering pirate John 'Calico Jack' Rackham, who seduced her with expensive baubles and offered to buy her from her husband, but James Bonny would have none of it.

Rackham decided that the only way he could keep Anne was to go back to pirating. They took over the *Curlew*, a merchant sloop that anchored in the harbour at New Providence. With Jack at the helm, the *Curlew* slipped out of the harbour.

They put into Cuba, where Anne gave birth. Leaving the infant there, they took to plundering coastal traders and fishing boats all around the Caribbean.

Taking a Dutch vessel, they forced a number of the crewmen to sign articles and join them. One of them, a handsome young boy, was very much to Anne's liking. When Jack caught them together, he threatened to kill them both.

The new crewmember turnded out to be an Englishwoman named Mary Read. She too was illegitimate and her mother, to disguise the fact, had dressed her as a boy. She served as a cabin boy on a man-o'-war and became a foot soldier before marrying. After her Flemish husband died of fever, she disguised herself as a sailor and signed on board the Dutch ship taken by Calico Jack.

In October 1720, the pirates of the *Curlew* swarmed on board a merchantman off Jamaica. Soon after, while the pirates were celebrating, they were challenged by a privateer from Jamaica. The men were too drunk to fight and cowered in the hold, while Anne and Mary fought off the boarders with pistols, cutlasses and boarding axes. But eventually they were overpowered.

The pirates were tried in Spanish Town, Jamaica. Calico Jack, Anne, Mary and eight other crewmen were found guilty and sentenced to be hanged, but the two women were pregnant, and, under English law, no court had the power to condemn an unborn child, no matter how guilty the mother.

Mary Read died of white fever in prison and Calico Jack was hanged in Jamaica. After Anne Bonny gave birth, her wealthy father bought her release. Still not yet 20, she became the mistress of Robert Fenwick, a former Red Sea pirate, who lived in South Carolina. Later she ran away with a young lover, but Fenwick caught up with them. He forced her to help hang the lover and promise never to run away again.

Other cross-dressers

The eighteenth century was full of cross-dressers, some of whom achieved minor celebrity in England.

There was Christian Davis (1667–1739), who was wounded serving as a dragoon in Marlborough's army at the Battle of Ramillies in 1706. Phoebe Hessel (c. 1713–1821) was a private in the Northumberland Fusiliers, and was wounded at Fontenoy in 1743. A street was named after her in Whitechapel. Hannah Snell (1723–92) sailed to India as a Royal Marine and fought at the Battle of Pondicherry in 1748, where she was wounded. Two years later she revealed that she was a woman and received a pension from the Duke of Cumberland. She married twice and raised two sons. In 1791 she was admitted to the Bedlam lunatic asylum, where she died six months later.

At 15 Mary Anne Talbot (1778–1808) was a drummer boy captured at the Battle of Valenciennes. Then, at 16, she was a powder monkey on board the *Brunswick* at the Battle of Ushant in 1794, the first great naval engagement of the French Revolutionary wars.

A black woman calling herself 'William Brown' joined the Royal Navy and concealed her sex for 11 years, rising to become captain of the fore-top on the 110-gun *Queen Charlotte* during the Napoleonic Wars.

The ladies of Llangollen

In the 1770s, two young ladies from prominent families in Ireland named Sarah Ponsonby and Lady Eleanor Butler developed a passionate friendship. When their relatives ob-jected, they fled to Wales, where they set up home together in the market town of Llangollen.

According to the *St James's Chronicle* of 17–20 July 1790, Lady Eleanor was 'tall and masculine', while Sarah was 'effeminate, fair and beautiful'. The *Chronicle*'s article was headed EXTRAORDINARY FEMALE AFFECTION, but there was no suggestion that anything untoward was taking place.

Same-sex marriage

On 1 October 1747, John Ferren and Deborah Nolan of St Andrew's Holborn underwent a Fleet marriage. 'The supposed John Ferren was discovered after the ceremony was over to be in person a woman,' the Fleet register records.

One same-sex couple lived together for 36 years, running a pub in Poplar. Their deception was only discovered when the 'wife' died, bequeathing half their joint property to the 'husband'. The dead woman's family contested the will. Faced with litigation the 'widower' confessed to being a woman.

Game at flatts

On 5 July 1777, a woman was put in the pillory at Cheapside and sent to prison for six months for dressing as a man and marrying three women, concurrently. On each occasion, she robbed and deserted them. According to the author of *Satan's Harvest Home*, this was a 'new kind of sin', which he called the 'game at flatts'. It was, he said, as common among the ladies of Twickenham as it was in the bathhouses of Turkey and a visitor from Germany hinted that tribadism was widespread among the schoolgirls of the period.

'These inexperienced young creatures,' he wrote in 1799, 'full of sensuality, are left together without any supervision whatever, especially when they are in bed, and spend their time reading obscene novels or in even more shameful amusements that are unmentionable.'

Anandrinic societies

Another German visitor mentioned the existence of tribade clubs in London around that time.

'There is no limit to the libidinousness in London,' he said:

There are females who avoid all intimate intercourse with the opposite sex, confining themselves to their own sex. They have small societies, known as Anandrinic Societies, of which Mrs Y—, formerly a famous London actress [thought to be Mary Anne Yates of the Drury Lane Theatre], was one of their presidents. These women offer up their unclean sacrifices at these places, but their altars are not worthy of the secret groves where Dionne's doves were united in love; all they deserve is a thick veil to obscure them from the sight of men.

Anandrinic, it should be noted, derives from the Greek word for impotence.

Dildos

'Dil-dols' were in great demand in the eighteenth century. A contemporary account records that a Mrs Philips had a shop that sold nothing but 'wares which are never sold publicly, which indeed can hardly be found at all in ordinary towns, and are only made and used in London and Paris'.

In his survey of prostitution in London, Michael Ryan said that they were used in brothels. They were made of India rubber and could be bought for £2 10s – £160 at today's prices.

Advanced varieties were on the market in Victorian England. There were double-ended dildos that could be used by two women at the same time. Others had two prongs that penetrated the vagina and anus simultaneously. Another had an attachment for the chin. And there was a astonishing amount of literature telling a young ladies how to use one.

Love and Safety, published in 1908, suggested taking a large carriage candle and carving it into the shape of a penis. Carrots and long eau-de-cologne bottles should not be used because they might cause injury due to their hardness.

'Obigees' on sale in Covent Garden were also good and, for younger women, a banana could be used. It also recommended going to a surgical instrument maker and purchasing a rectal bougie. These needed to be warmed in hot water before use.

Hermaphrodites

A cattle drover named Bob Bussicks, who died in London in 1792, was a hermaphrodite who became one of the sights of the city. It is said that he was the inspiration behind the pornographic classic *Letters from Laura and Eveline, giving an Account of their Mock Marriage, Wedding Trip, etc.*, published in London in 1883.

In it, Laura and Eveline are hermaphrodites, who can take both active and passive roles in sex. They get married simultaneously and their husbands, though surprised, are not displeased to find that they have male sexual organs as well as female ones. The nuptials are celebrated by an orgy at a London club with numerous ladies and gentleman and every possible permutation.

Sappho on stage

According to English sexologist Henry Havelock Ellis, at the end of the nineteenth century lesbianism was widespread in the big London theatres and music halls. A friend reported that passionate friendships between girls are very common among the actresses, chorus and ballet girls, especially the ballet girls: crowded dressing rooms provided 'ample opportunities for the development of such emotional aberrations'.

A question of class

Lower and middle classes were governed by tradition and conventional ideas and did not usually indulge, noted Havelock Ellis. But lesbianism was not uncommon among the upper classes, who had more freedom and less prejudice. It was also practised by the better class of prostitute.

'A considerable number of well-known prostitutes are reputed to have a homosexual tendency,' reported Ellis's informant, 'but this does not affect their attitude towards their profession. I do not know of any prostitute who confines herself exclusively to lesbianism …'. The informant spoke of

hints to the effect that there have been one or two such abnormal creatures. One night I visited the Corinthian Club (a locale frequented by better-class prostitutes) and heard a fashionably dressed prostitute announcing that she would go home with a girl, and no one present doubted her word …. But among the lower-class prostitutes such practices are extremely rare.

Lesbianism and the law

It is widely held that the Protection of Women and Suppression of Brothels Bill of 1885 originally all made acts of 'gross indecency' between members of the same sex a punishable offence. But, when presented to Queen Victoria, she is supposed to have said, 'Women don't do such things.' So any reference to Sapphic love was removed. There is no record of this.

In another version of the story, lesbianism was excluded

from the Bill because no one was willing to explain it to her. This too seems implausible. Victoria may have been conservative in social matters, but she had lived too long and was far too inquisitive to have remained an innocent. She was, after all, a hot-blooded Hanoverian from a family whose depravity knew no bounds.

There was clearly another reason why lesbianism has never been outlawed. When Conservative MP Frederick Macquister proposed an amendment to the 1885 Act covering 'gross indecency by females' in 1918, MPs blustered about the declining moral standards among women and its effect on the birth rate, and the House of Commons passed the motion. But in the House of Lords, Lord Birkenhead said, 'You are going to tell the whole world there is such an offence, to bring it to the notice of women who have never heard of it, never dreamed of it. I think this is a very great mischief.' The amendment foundered.

CHAPTER SIXTEEN

Defloration Mania

HE GERMAN SEXOLOGIST Ivan Bloch ascribed the English passion for virgins to the fact that, for the Englishman, only the best is good enough: 'He must have something that can be possessed only once and by only one person, which he can boast of to others.'

A want of virginity

The London financier Sir Horatio Palavinco, cohort of Elizabeth I's spymaster Sir Francis Walsingham, employed Gilbert Periam as a pimp. When Palavinco asked Periam to bring him a virgin, he was told that there were none available in London. So Palavinco gave Periam a horse and 10 shillings – 50p, or £90 at today's prices – to go to Guildford to find him one.

Followers of fashion

Until the end of the eighteenth century there was little demand for virgins in the sex trade of London. However, the trend seems to have begun with a pernicious little tome called *The Battles of Venus*, printed in the Hague in 1760 and ascribed to Voltaire. It was reprinted several times in London, where it lost its attribution.

'In truth I esteem the fruition of a virgin to be, with respect to the mind and body of the enjoyer, the highest aggravation of sensual delight,' wrote the author, who went on to describe in graphic detail the delights of defloration, recommending virgins of whom

> yet no ringlets deck the pouting mount, but all is like her lily hand, both bare and smooth, before the periodical lustration hath stained her virgin shift, whilst her bosom boasts only a general swell rather than distinct orbs, and whilst her tender mind is ignorant of what man can do unto her.

And he recommended visiting girls' boarding schools.

Although the author urges the protagonist to 'pity a tender virgin's sufferings', he actually extols rape:

> I cannot conceive a higher banquet to a man of lustful humour, than to see a modest and beautiful woman forcibly stripped naked: to observe her struggling and, and discording her hidden beauties by degree, until she comes to her last shift, and then to lay her down, and notwithstanding her efforts, rifle all her charms, and penetrate even into her honeyed treasure.

The virgin's resistance and her cries of pain 'produce an emission copious, rapid and transporting', he writes, and part of the delight

> arises from considering that the lewdest part of your body is fixed in the delicious centre of her body, that you feel the convulsive wrigglings of the chaste nymph you have so long adored, and at last feel her diffuse her warm juice throughout her dewy sheath, and moisten the hot, ruby crest of your firm-fixed instrument.

Virgin mad

The demand for virgins reached its height in the 1880s. The campaigning editor of the *Pall Mall Gazette*, W.T. Stead, found a doctor in London who deflowered three virgins in a fortnight. And the Russian anthropologist Professor Benjamin Tarnowsky reported in *Prostitution and Abolitionism* that there was one man in England who went through 70 virgins in a year, but would happily have made it a 100, given the opportunity.

Virginity restored

As demand grew, brothels had a problem. Each new girl was good for one trip only. So doctors were called in to see if they could somehow restore a girl's virginity and they turned to Arabian medical writings from the Middle Ages to discover how to do it.

There were two main components to the process. The first was to simulate some blood flow during penetration as if the hymen were being torn. This was achieved by putting a blood-filled fish bladder or blood-soaked sponge into the vagina before intercourse. Worse, a leech could be inserted so that, when an eager lover dislodged it, blood would run. Worse still – excruciatingly so – was inserting pieces of broken glass.

Next, the passage itself had to be tightened. An astringent decoction of sloes or acorns, cypress nuts, Provençal roses, myrrh and other styptics were used as a method by which 'the normal female parts, now too wide, may be drawn together'. Otherwise the steam produced when a heated brick or a red-hot iron was dropped into vinegar was applied.

The genuine article?

When one Alderman Portsoken expressed his surprise at coming across a genuine virgin in Charlotte Hayes's establishment in King's Place, London, the politician George Selwyn questioned her about it. Madame Hayes said it was perfectly possible for a woman to lose her virginity 500 times and continue to pass as a virgin. She herself, she said, had had her virginity restored a thousand times by a Dr O' Patrick.

Child prostitution

The demand for virgins led to an increase in child prostitution. Foreign observers were horrified to see children selling themselves on the streets of Spitalfields and Bethnal Green in the daytime. At night they moved west.

In Crispin Street, Spitalfields, in 1810, there was a brothel that specialised in girls under 14. By the 1830s, it had competition from Catherine Keeley's in Dock Street, Maxwell's in Batty Street and numerous other establishments in Mile End Road and Bedford Square (East). John Jacobs's place in New Norfolk Street offered girls of 12 and one 10-year-old was found on the premises.

These places catered to a child clientele as well. On a Saturday evening, a little girl would be sent out to collect 14 boys aged 10 to 15 and bring them back to the brothel. When she had collected enough boys who, between them, could pay the tariff, the young girl and two juvenile companions would take them on. This way the brothel built its future clientele.

Sometimes the boys could be seduced into prostitution themselves. William Sheen of Algar Place, Wentworth Street, Spitalfields, ran 'pornological clubs', where men and women had sex with the children he provided. He always had 30 to 40 boys and girls aged 9 to 18 to hand. When the Society for the Suppression of Vice succeeded in closing these places down, the inmates who could not be returned to their friends or family were sent to an asylum.

Maiden tribute

W.T. Stead set up a 'secret commission' to investigate child prostitution, which reported in a series of five articles in the *Pall Mall Gazette* in July 1885 called 'The Maiden Tribute of Modern Babylon'. It found there was a whole industry involved in procuring, certifying and selling virgins.

A brothel owner, who himself had married a 14-year-old prostitute, told Stead: 'Maids, as you call them – fresh girls as we know them in the trade – are constantly in request, and a keeper who knows his business has his eyes open in all directions ...'. He tells how he has

> gone and courted girls in the country under all kinds of disguises, occasionally assuming the dress of a parson, and made them believe that I intended to marry them, and so got them in my power to please a good customer. How is it done? Why, after courting my girl for a time, I propose to bring her to London to see the sights.

She would be wined and dined and taken to the theatre but it would be contrived that she would miss her last train and would be offered lodgings. The brothel owner described how 'she goes to bed in my house, and then the affair is managed. My client gets his maid, I get my £10 or £20 commission [£700 or £1,400 today], and in the morning the girl, who has lost her character, and dare not go home ...'

From then on she would likely make her living as the others did, and become one of his 'marks', bringing trade to the brothel. The brothel owner – who sent his own daughter on to the streets – told Stead that another way of supplying girls was by breeding them: many women on the streets had female children, who would eventually 'become merchantable' and may sell for £20 or £40 (£1,400 or £2,800 today). Drunken parents would also often sell their children to brothel keepers.

Miss X and Miss Z

The most infamous providers of virgins were W.T. Stead's informants, Miss X and Miss Z.

'The difference between the firm of Mesdames X. and Z. and the ordinary keeper of an introducing house is that the procuring of maids (which in the case of the latter is occasional) is the constant occupation of their lives,' said Stead. 'They do nothing else. They keep no house of ill-fame.'

One of the members of 'this remarkable firm' lived with her parents, the other in lodgings, he wrote, the latter holding down a position of trust and influence with a firm in Oxford Street. 'These things, however, are but as blinds. Their real work, to which they devote every day in the week, is the purveying of maidens to an extensive and ever-widening circle of customers …'

The business was begun by Miss X when she was 15 and was herself procured by an established prostitute. She saw how easy it was to make money at it. After two years in the business, she took on Miss Z as a partner.

The two women specialised in recruiting 'nurse-girls and shop-girls, although occasionally we get a governess, and sometimes cooks and other servants'. Young girls from the country, 'fresh and rosy', were picked up in the shops or when they were running errands.

The two women scoured the royal parks keeping 'a sharp look-out for any likely girl'. They would see her week after week 'until we are sufficiently in her confidence to suggest how easy it is to earn a few pounds by meeting a man … Thus we have always a crop of maids ripening, and at any time we can undertake to deliver a maid if we get due notice.'

Miss X and Miss Z avoided telling the girls any explicit details of what they were in for. Some were very naïve and found even undressing an ordeal. There were those who knew what was going to happen, others would grow frightened when they were confronted with the sex act itself. In that case Misses X and Z would hold the poor girl down while their client raped her. Other procuresses used a 'drowse' or a 'black draught' of laudanum or chloroform, so the girl was unconscious when she was deflowered.

But for some men this was not good enough. 'In my house, you can enjoy the screams of the girl with the certainty that no one else hears them but yourself,' a seemingly respectable woman brothel keeper told Stead. 'Flogging, both of men and women, goes on regularly in ordinary rooms, but the cry of the bleeding subject never attracts attention from the outside world …. To some men, however, the shriek of torture is the essence of their delight, and they would not silence by a single note the cry of agony over which they gloat.'

Certificate of virginity

Brothel owners supplied a certificate of virginity with the girls they procured. It was possible to bribe a doctor to supply bogus certificates, but Miss X and Miss Z saw no reason to do that, since the supply of virgins was plentiful.

W.T. Stead put them to the test, ordering five virgins at £5 – £350 today – per maidenhead. The girl would get half of this. Stead told the women that he was buying these girls wholesale with the intention of selling on their chastity. The going rate for a virgin at that time was £10 (£700 today) in the East End and a whopping £20 (£1,400) in the West End.

When the two procuresses arrived with the first batch of three, Stead accompanied them to the doctor, where they submitted to examination, one by one, without objection. Some naïve girls mistook the examination for the act itself.

'To the unutterable disgust of the girls two of them were refused a certificate,' wrote Stead. 'The doctor could not say that they were not virgins; but neither of them was technically a *virgo intacta*. I then gave them 5s. [£17.50] per head for their trouble.' The other girl was given a written certificate, which proclaimed her a virgin.

The following Monday, two nursemaids were taken to the doctor's and certified as virgins. The next Friday, taking no chances, Miss X and Miss Z turned up with four more girls –

three of them were 14, the other 18. Only the 18-year-old was certified.

'It is always the young ones who are unable to stand the doctor's examination,' rued Miss X.

The girls who had been certified were then required to sign a document agreeing to surrender their newly confirmed virginity. 'I hereby agree to let you have me for £5, and will come to any address you send me at two days' notice,' it read.

If the girls were underage, they would also have to get a certificate signed by one of their parents saying that they consented to their 'seduction'. It was a common way for working-class families to make a bit of money.

Miss X and Miss Z went to all this trouble because of the competition from girls whose virginity had been 'restored'. They were so plentiful that the market for uncertificated virginity was depressed.

The crusade

The *Pall Mall Gazette*'s investigation of Victorian child prostitution caused a stir. A committee of the great and the good – including the Archbishop of Canterbury – was set up and found that Stead's exposé was correct in its essentials.

Stead then began a crusade. Some 250,000 people turned out for a rally in Hyde Park in August 1885. However, along with members of religious organisations, in the crowd were numerous prostitutes who used the gathering to solicit men. Religious and moral tracts were circulated, along with the pornographic journal the *Devil*, whose front page showed three ladies 'displaying their voluptuous charms'.

Soon afterwards, *Lloyd's News* carried the story of a mother who was searching for her daughter, 13-year-old Eliza Armstrong. Stead was accused of kidnapping the girl. She had been brought to him by an ex-prostitute named Jarett, who had her certified by a midwife as a virgin and chloroformed. Stead was in the room at the time, it was said. He had then taken her to Paris, where he handed her over to the Salvation Army.

Stead and his companions – including William Booth, founder of the Salvation Army – were prosecuted. After a long and detailed trial, Stead was sentenced to three months' imprisonment. On his release, he continued his career in campaigning journalism. He died on board the *Titanic* and was last seen reading quietly in the first-class smoking room as the ship went down.

CHAPTER SEVENTEEN

The English Vice

HE FRENCH CALL IT '*le vice Anglais*' and it is
practically unknown in Italy and Spain. Only the
English, it seems, find erotic pleasure in the act
of spanking. What is all the more remarkable is
that the fashion for flagellation reached its height among the
middle and upper classes at a time when flogging was inflicted
extensively on the lower classes as punishment.

Whipping the wench

In the sixteenth century, poet, dramatist and spy Christopher
Marlowe (1564–93) described his own longings in this quarter:

> When Francis comes to solace with his whore,
> He sends for rods and strips himself stark naked;
> For his lust sleeps, and will not rise before
> By whipping of the wench it be awaked.
> I envy him not, but wish I had the power,
> To make myself his wench but one half-hour.

Whipping Tom

Towards the end of the seventeenth century, the streets of London were haunted by an individual known as Whipping Tom, who would truss, slap or whip any woman he met. He was so adroit at evading capture that it was thought he was endowed with supernatural powers.

In 1681, a book was published about him. It was called *Whipping Tom Brought to light, and exposed to View: In an Account of several late Adventures of the pretended Whipping Spirit.*

'Whipping Tom,' it said, 'for some weeks, has lurked about in alleys and courts in Fleet-street, Chancery-lane, Shoe-lane, Fetter-lane, the Strand, Holborn, and other places, and at unawares seizes upon such as he can conveniently make light on, and turning them up as nimble as an eel, makes their butt ends cry *spanko* … and then vanishes.'

Tom is said to have seized a servant girl out looking for her master, 'and in a trice, laying her cross his knee, took up her linen and lay'd so hard upon her backside as made her cry out most piteously for help …'

Eventually a man named Thomas Wallis was arrested and tried for 'not only taking up women's coats and viewing their nakedness, and exposing many a pretty female's backside to the

extremity of the wind and rainy weather; but even then in a violent and unmerciful way lashed their tender buttocks, hips and thighs, both within and without'.

He pleaded not guilty on the grounds that women deserved to be 'whip'd out of their wickedness', otherwise men would become their slaves. However, a specially selected all-woman jury found him guilty of 'oppression and tyranny'. He was sentenced to be 'whip'd twice a week in Bridewell by two maids, with each a birch rod, till the blood on his back comes in six places; and this to be continued for one whole year'.

He also had to stand in the pillory three times – at the Temple Bar, the Royal Exchange and Margaret's Hill in Southwark – and, at the end of the 12 months, 'to run the gauntlet through two hundred maids, wives and widows in Cheapside, and to give security for his good behaviour for seven years, and fined 2,000 marks, and not to be discharged from imprisonment till the money is paid'.

Bloody assizes

Judge Jeffreys, who sentenced 320 people to hang at the Bloody Assizes of 1685, was known for his sadism and delighted sentencing people – particularly women – to flogging. Macaulay wrote in his *History of England*,

> There was a fiendish exultation in the way in which he pronounced sentence on offenders. Their weeping and imploring seemed to titillate him voluptuously; and he loved to scare them into fits by dilating with luxuriant amplification on all the details of what they were to suffer. Thus, when he had the opportunity of ordering an unlucky adventuress to

be whipped at the cart's tail, 'Hangman,' he would exclaim, 'I charge you to pay particular attention to this lady! Scourge her soundly, man. Scourge her till the blood runs down! It is Christmas, a cold time for Madam to strip in! See that you warm her shoulders thoroughly!'

Flagellomania

Throughout the eighteenth century, beating for sexual pleasure became a craze that spawned its own literature.

Stories about flagellation occurred regularly in magazines such as the *Rambler's*, the *Original Rambler's* and *Bon Ton*. *Notes and Queries* carried pages of letters on the subject. And letters of the topic of flagellation filled the pages of the *Family Herald* and the *Englishwoman's Domestic Magazine*. These were so popular that letters that appeared between April and December 1870 were published as a separate pamphlet called *Letters addressed to the Editor of the Englishwoman's Domestic Magazine on the Whipping of Girls*. It begins, 'I have read with much pleasure your manly and outspoken remarks on the subject of "Indecent Whipping of Girls" ...' The letters largely focus on the fact that the young women in question, some 18 or 20, were publicly stripped naked – often in front of men – for the punishment to be performed. Afterwards they had to kneel down and kiss the rod.

Soon afterwards, the 550-page *History of the Rod in all countries from the earliest period to the present time ... with illustrations*, by the Reverend William M. Cooper, was published and quickly sold out. In it, Cooper related the strange tale of a nobleman in the reign of George II who hired a house in London with a pretty young housekeeper. Once a week she hired two other servants. The nobleman would then pretend to be a girl from a poor house who did her chores so badly that the other women had to whip him.

Devotees of the rod

The German sexologist Ivan Bloch noted that the passion for flagellation in England was not confined to old men or those 'exhausted by sexual perversion'. Young men and those in the prime of life also indulged. *Venus's Schoolmistress; or Birchen Sports* of 1788 said that 'generals, admirals, colonels, captains, bishops, judges, barristers, lords, members of the House of Commons and doctors were all devotees of the rod'.

Many women also participated. A gentleman, himself a passionate devotee of the birch, writing in 1877, said, 'In my experience I have known personally several ladies of high rank who had an extraordinary passion for administering the rod, and that too with merciless severity.'

He said he knew of only one who liked receiving it, 'and she was quite of the lowest order'. When she was drunk, 'she would allow herself to be birched until her bottom was utterly raw, and the rod saturated with blood, she crying out during the operation "Harder! Harder!" and blaspheming if it was not well laid on'.

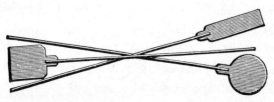

The foreign view

The French put the English penchant for flagellation down to excessive drinking, while the Germans saw it as the perfectly natural expression of sexual sadism, pointing out that certain expressions, movements and colour changes induced by flagellation resembled those arising in the sexual acts. Consequently they were stimulating for both the giver and the receiver.

In his *History of the Flagellants, or the Advantages of Discipline*, Jean Louis de Lolme of Geneva said the sexual flagellation in its most usually practised form, the whipping of the posterior, was encouraged by the purely aesthetic charm of the backside. A particular turn-on, gentlemen found, was the reddening of the buttocks after a sound thrashing. Then there was their orgasmic quivering as they were beaten.

Varieties of flagellants

Venus's Schoolmistress; or Birchen Sports said that male flagellants were divided into three types: (1) those who liked to receive more or less severe chastisement from the hand of a woman who took pleasure in wielding the rod with power and skill; (2) those who liked to apply the rod to a female; and (3) those who liked to watch.

Female flagellants could be divided up in exactly the same way.

Mistresses of the rod

Brothels specialising in flagellation in London started in 1760 with Mrs Jenkins's establishment. By 1800, there were many of them. In the introduction of his index of prohibited books, Pisanus Fraxi said:

> At the early part of this century very sumptuously fitted up establishments exclusively devoted to the administration of the birch were not uncommon in London; and women of the town served, as it were, an apprenticeship in order to acquire the art of gracefully and effectively administering the rod.

According to Fraxi, many of these women took a passionate interest in their calling. 'It would be easy to form a lengthy list of these female flagellants, but I shall restrict myself to the mention of a few only.'

First on his shortlist is Mrs Collett, who was a 'noted whipper' who numbered among her clients George IV. She ran an establishment in Tavistock Court, Covent Garden, later in Portland Place and Bedford Street, off Russell Square. When she died, her niece Mrs Mitchell took over the business and moved it to 22, then 44, Waterloo Road, then finally to St Mary's Square, Kennington.

Mrs James, the one-time maid of Lord Clanricade, ran a house at 7 Carlisle Street, Soho, which was so successful that she acquired a substantial fortune before she retired to live in luxury in Notting Hill, 'her house being decorated with pictures and her person covered with jewels'.

School of Flogging

In July 1863, under the auspices of the Society for the Protection of Females, Mrs Stewart's 'academy' was raided by the police and, according to Pisanus Fraxi, a 'rare collection of flagellation appurtenances' was taken to Westminster Police Court. These 'curious instruments of her stock-in-trade consisted of a folding ladder with straps, birch rods, furze brooms and secret implements for the use of male and female'; and she was accused of 'decoying young females into Stewart's School of Flogging, to undergo the ordeal of the birch from old and young flagellists, for the benefit of the woman Stewart'.

During the ensuing court case a pamphlet was produced with the unwieldy title *Mysteries of Flagellation or, A History of the Secret Ceremonies of the Society of Flagellants. The Saintly Practice of the Birch! St Francis whipped by the Devil! How to subdue the Passions by the Art of Flogging! With many Curious Anecdotes of the Prevalence of this Peculiar Pastime in all Nations and Epochs, whether Savage or Civilised*. It said of the Stewart case that her method of conducting business was to 'get hold of young girls, board, lodge, and clothe them'. In return, the girls were obliged to administer to the lusts of the patrons.

They were flogged in different ways. Some strapped to the ladder, at others flogged round the room – at times they were laid on the bed. Every device or variation which perverted ingenuity could devise was resorted to, to give variety to the orgies, in return for which the mistress of the house was paid sums varying from £5 to £15.

Worth £300 to £900 at today's prices, those sums enabled Stewart to keep a country house and a fancy man, to the great scandal of the community.

Pisanus Fraxi (author of an index of prohibited books), said that this account of what went on at Mrs Stewart's establishment was exaggerated and he attempted to put the record straight, saying,

> It cannot be said that the girl was flogged against her will, for she was in the habit of birching gentlemen, and even of submitting to be whipped herself when well paid. The flagellations which went on under her auspices were chiefly administered to gentlemen, although girls were of course at times castigated.

Nevertheless Mrs Stewart was convicted of beating a girl against her will and sent to prison. Afterwards she lived in Howland Street, where she was convicted of selling indecent books. After that, her fortunes declined. She moved to the Old Kent Road, then to Lavinia Grove, King's Cross, where she died in 1873.

Fraxi concluded: 'Were it not indiscreet, I might add the names of one or two other ladies who still carry on their calling.'

Queen of the rod

Pisanus Fraxi named as 'queen of the profession' Mrs Theresa Berkley of 28 Charlotte Street, Portland Place. She was, he said, 'a perfect mistress of her art' and understood how to satisfy her clients. She was also an accomplished businesswoman who amassed a considerable fortune during her career.

Mrs Berkley possessed the first grand requisite for a courtesan, said Fraxi – lewdness.

> She would study every lech, whim, caprice, and desire of her customer, and had the disposition to gratify them, if her avarice was rewarded in return. Her instruments of torture were more numerous than those of any other governess. Her supply of birch was extensive, and kept in water, so that it was always green and pliant …

She had several, with a dozen thongs on each, as well as a dozen different sizes of cat-o'-nine tails, 'some with needle points worked into them'. There were also 'various kinds of thin bending canes; leather straps like coach traces; battledoors [bats or paddles] made of thick sole-leather with inch nails run through to docket, and currycomb round hides rendered callous by many years of flagellation'.

On the second floor of her establishment in Charlotte Street, there was also a pulley system, where a man could be suspended by his hands. 'Thus, at her shop, whoever went with plenty of money, could be birched, whipped, fustigated [cudgelled], scourged, needle-pricked, half-hung, holly-brushed, furze-brushed, butcher-brushed, stinging-nettled, curry-combed, phlebotomised [made to bleed], and tortured till he had had a bellyful.'

If a man wanted to beat a woman, Mrs Berkley herself would submit to a certain extent – 'but if they were gluttons at it, she had women in attendance who would take any number of lashes the flogger pleased'.

The Berkley horse

In the spring of 1828 Mrs Berkley introduced a special apparatus for a gentlemen to be flogged on. Known as the 'Berkley horse' or *chevalet*, it presented the body in any position desired. A print of the device appeared in her memoirs *The Favourite of Venus, or Secrets of My Note Book Explained in the Life of a Votary of Pleasure*. It showed a naked man strapped in position.

'A woman is sitting in a chair exactly under it with her bosom, belly and bush exposed: she is manualising his *embolon*, while Mrs Berkley is birching his posteriors,' said Fraxi.

The services of Mrs Berkley were in great demand. In January 1836, a young man wrote to her at her Charlotte Street address, saying he was 'a badly behaved young man and quite incorrigible!' and admitting that 'the most celebrated tutors in London' had chastised him but had been unable to curb his wilfulness. After recounting a number of places recommended to him, he went on to say,

Finally, honoured lady, I received an introduction from your close friend, Count G., which is causing me to jump for joy, because I have been told of your famous apparatus, the *chevalet,* which should succeed in punishing sufficiently undisciplined young men like myself.

He offered to see her 'at the beginning of February, when I am in London with my friend the Count, where parliamentary duties await us' (no change here, then), and then listed his requirements:

- It is necessary that I should be securely fastened to the *chevalet* with chains that I will bring myself.

- A pound sterling for the first blood drawn.

- Two pounds sterling if blood runs down to my heels.

- Three pounds sterling if my heels are bathed in blood.

- Four pounds sterling if the blood reaches the floor.

- Five pounds sterling if you succeed in making me lose consciousness.

When Mrs Berkley died later in 1836, her original horse was presented to the Society of Arts in the Adelphi by her executor. She left £10,000, amassed over eight years. This was bequeathed to her brother, a missionary in Australia. But, when he arrived in London and discovered how it had been earned, he renounced all claim and the money was forfeit to the crown.

By the time of Paris Exhibition of 1900, the *chevalet* had found favour in France – another great British export.

The whipping machines

In the eighteenth century, the English roué Chace Price designed a machine that could flagellate 40 people at a time. He discussed the matter with the actor Samuel Foote in Charlotte Hayes's establishment and Price was eager to get it patented.

A multiple thrashing machine was seen in operation in a London brothel by James Beard Talbot in 1830. Then an industrial college in Denver, Colorado, took the English vice and added electricity. A report talks of the 'contrivance in question' as a chair with no seat, which the 'patient' sits on, having uncovered his backside.

This up-to-date chair is sufficiently raised to allow four beaters fixed beneath it to operate freely in a rotatory movement, faster or slower according to the operator, who has only to switch on an electric battery fixed to the chair with metal wires. The beaters, set in motion, do their job most conscientiously, and possess the advantage of working in a regulated, orderly manner without the least fatigue to the operator.

The purpose of chastisement

In old England there was a great deal of discussion about what flagellation was for. Some purists maintained that it was an end in itself. Pisanus Fraxi disagreed.

'Flagellation,' he said, 'if it has any value, is a preparation for a higher pleasure (for it can scarcely be called a pleasure itself), a means to an end, not the end itself.' For him it was a violent form of foreplay.

The weight of medical opinion was on his side. In *Aphrodisiacs and Anti-Aphrodisiacs* (1869), John Davenport said, 'It is impossible to doubt that flagellation exercised upon the buttocks and the adjacent parts has a powerful effect upon the organs of generation.'

Arab doctors, it was said, prescribed flagellation for impotence and infertility. Italians thought it increased a woman's chances of conception. Persians and Russians both thrashed their wives before performing their conjugal duties, and it was said that a Russian wife measured how much her husband loved her by the number of strokes he applied.

It was also thought that, by bringing the blood to the affected parts, birching helped develop larger buttocks – a desirable quality in the age of the bustle.

Other delights

The erotic brochure *On the Venusburg* recommended rubbing powdered asbestos into the skin to induce a prickling and burning sensation – much like being whipped but without so much damage to the skin. They did not know then, of course, of the carcinogenic properties of asbestos.

And in *Lascivious Gems*, published in London in 1866, a lady tied her impotent lover to a bedpost and beat him with a rod.

'Still I was not satiated,' she said, hardly surprisingly. 'Seizing a hand-brush, I struck the raw flesh with the bristles and scrubbed it with them. I then took the eau-de-cologne bottle from the dressing table and poured the contents onto the parts and resumed the use of the hair-brush.'

The poor man passed out.

The high-born governess

According to *Venus's Schoolmistress*, the governess who handed out the beating had to be an experienced woman, made perfect in the art. 'She must possess a quick and intense method, to recognise the various aberrations of men's fancy, and show instant readiness to meet and satisfy them.'

Margaret Anson, the author of *The Merry Order of St Bridget* published in London in 1857, said,

> There is no enjoyment either in the use or endurance of the rod when it is vulgarly used, like a woman would strike in passion; but when an elegant, high-bred woman wields it with dignity of mien and grace of attitude, then both the practice and the suffering become a real pleasure.

Nosegays

Prostitutes wore nosegays pinned to the bodices on the street as a sign that they provided flagellation. These were known as the 'nosegays of lechery' and were seen in the eighteenth century adorning the bosoms of women at Vauxhall and Ranelagh Gardens.

Cut-up

Some Englishmen took the practice of flagellation one step further with the notorious 'cut-up', which involves the beating of the genitals and perineum. *The Romance of Chastisement, or the Revelations of Miss Darcy*, published in London, describes it, as does the more originally titled *With Rod and Bum; or Sport in the West End of London by Ophelia Cox. A true tale by a young governess of 1898.*

Watching

Other men and women joined in the flagellomania merely by watching. One old man paid a police agent a ducat to watch every time a prostitute who had been arrested was flogged.

Another police officer put on events where dozens of young women were beaten both on their backs and their bare buttocks. Society ladies turned up to watch the spectacle. In one case, he ordered 20 servant girls who had been out on the streets after eight o'clock to be flogged unmercifully.

The officer was finally disgraced when, in polite society, he handed a lady a pinch of snuff and she saw, inside the lid of his snuff box, the picture of a young woman being beaten.

Female flagellation clubs

In the eighteenth century, there were female flagellation clubs. One met every Thursday in Jermyn Street. *Bon Ton* of December 1792 carried a detail description of the goings-on there, describing the members as mainly married women who wanted to reawaken the ecstasy they experienced at the beginning of their married life. After a speech on the effects of flagellation, six 'patients' took their places and the demonstration began, said the magazine.

The president of the club hands out stout rods and begins the chastisement herself, 'with any variation she likes while the others watch'. Sometimes, she would order that the whipping start on the calves and rise to the posterior, 'until the whole region, as Shakespeare says, from milk-white "becomes one red". After the president, the other flagellants take their turn.'

There were also 'juvenile flagellation clubs' where a forfeit game was played which involved the removal of clothing garment by garment, followed by the application of the rod.

Lectures

The *Sublime of Flagellation* was a pamphlet published in London in 1872. At the back it carried a 'Card Addressed to Gentleman Flagellants', introducing them to certain 'lectures'.

Those expressing interest would be 'referred to a lady of distinguished personal and mental accomplishments, who, on the proper compliment being made her, will deliver any one of the lectures, with all the eloquence and energy of impassioned voice and action happily united'.

The description continued,

The lady has a house of her own, and her LECTURE ROOM is furnished with rods, cat-o'-nine-tails, and some of the best prints of flagellation. The lady has a stout woman in her house, able to take a man on her back, when he chooses to be treated like a school-boy; and she and her maid are willing to be passive sometimes in the use of the rods, when required.

And there was an 'NB':

Single gentlemen, who are fond of representing school-boys, waited on by mistress and maid at any hour, before they are up in the morning, at their own houses, where the delightful divertissement of being taken out of bed, horsed and whipt, for not going to school, will be played to admiration.

These passive flagellants, known as 'flogging cullies', seem to have been in the majority, but others had a distinctly sadistic bent. One 'Colonel Spanker' delivered an 'experimental lecture' on the 'exciting and voluptuous pleasures to be derived from crushing and humiliating the spirit of a beautiful and modest young lady at the assembly room of the Society of Aristocratic Flagellants in Mayfair'.

According to Colonel Spanker, 'no enjoyment can be found in whipping the callous posterior of a match girl, who has been used to the rude corrections of her parents, but only from exposing the delicate nakedness of a real tenderly nurtured lady, whose mind has been carefully cultured'.

Public school

There can be little doubt that the English predilection for beating came from boarding schools, where children of both sexes were beaten. Westminster School was most notorious for the beatings its pupils received, with two junior staff being employed as 'rod makers'. In 1838, an attempt was made to curb the widespread use of birching, but the practice continued unabated and it is easy to see why it made such an impression on the burgeoning sexuality of youngsters.

On 13 March 1859 a gentleman wrote, fondly,

> In my boyish days it was customary in preparatory schools to have boys and girls together under a woman, and where the rod was used on all occasions with the utmost severity. We used to be birched in the presence of each other, girls across the knee, or held under the arm, the boys on the back of a maid servant.

Settled by the rod

In the late nineteenth century, a correspondent wrote to *Society* magazine, saying he endorsed the opinion of a previous correspondent with regard to 'the reciprocal punishment of man and wife; family discords of many sorts can be easily avoided thereby'.

Furthermore, he thought it was 'a wonderful excuse for the renewal of old healing remedies – the kissing habit, etc. There is a unique attraction in whipping one's own wife or in being whipped by her hand. I hope that the time will come when all quarrels will be settled by the rod.'

Strangulation

There was a fad for erotic strangulation in the late eighteenth century. It first surfaces in Jonathan Swift's *A Discourse concerning the Mechanical Operation of the Spirit* in 1710, where he mentions 'swinging by Session upon a Cord, in order to raise artificial extasies'. This, he said, was practised by women. But the sexual possibilities of hanging for men became known to the wider public with the death of the prominent Czech musician Francis Kotzwarra.

Kotzwarra came to England in 1769 and became an instant star, but soon he began to neglect his talent and slipped into a life of dissipation. At about one o'clock on the afternoon of 2 September 1791, he visited a prostitute in Covent Garden named Susannah Hill and asked her to have a drink with him. Later they went back to her room, where, she said, 'a number of most indecent acts took place'.

During their time together, he asked her to 'tear his genital organ in two' – which she refused. Then he said that he would like to be hanged for five minutes and gave her money to buy the rope. This, he said, would increase his pleasure and 'produce the desired effect'. She bought two thin cords and placed them around his neck, tying the other end to a door. He then drew up his legs, so that he was suspended by the neck. After about five minutes she cut him down. He fell on the floor. She thought he had fainted and called a woman living opposite for help. They tried to revive him, but failed.

Susannah Hill was arrested. A grand jury deliberated from five in the evening to two the following morning and eventually indicted her for 'wilful murder' on the grounds that this would discourage other women from co-operating in such deviant sexual practices. But, when the case came up at the Old Bailey on 16 September 1791, the judge ruled that her act was not premeditated murder but accidental manslaughter, and she was released after being admonished to lead a better life.

Because of the immodest nature of the evidence, the judge had already cleared the courtroom of any women and, deciding that details of the case were dangerous to public morality, he ordered all the documents relating to the case be destroyed. However, Susannah Hill published her own account in *Modern Propensities, or an essay on the Art of Strangling, &c., illustrated with several anecdotes. Bon Ton* of September 1793 picked up on it, publishing a review of Hill's pamphlet alongside an article on 'The Effects of Temporary Strangulation on the Human Body'. This pointed out that, a few seconds before Kotzwarra's death, Susannah Hill had observed 'certain signs which clearly proved the pleasant effect of this procedure'.

Kotzwarra's death did not discourage other thrill seekers. *Bon Ton* reported that in August 1793 a prominent citizen of Bristol had visited London and approached a pretty girl in Charlotte Street. He admitted to her that he was impotent but 'informed her of the method by which this evil could be eliminated, so that he might enjoy her lovely person to the full'.

The man stood on a low stool and threw the end of the rope over a beam, and 'with the aid of his fair companion, fastened it'. The stool was then removed and he was suspended so that his feet just touched the floor.

'Within thirty seconds the stimulating effect of this peculiar procedure was clearly in evidence,' reported *Bon Ton*. 'But suddenly he began to show alarming symptoms, so that the girl quickly released her peculiar lover. But in order to revive him completely it was necessary to invoke the assistance of the Society for Reviving Drowned Persons.'

CHAPTER EIGHTEEN

Provocative Attire

 ASHION HAS ALWAYS sought to be a sexual stimulant for both sexes. Sometimes nudity is in vogue. At others, the entire body is covered so that even a flash of an unclothed ankle is considered provocative. Clothing is also used to shift erotic attention around the body. Breasts might be in fashion one season, then the buttocks, calf, neck, thigh or even the genital region.

Dress codes

The Anglo-Saxons persisted in wearing primitive Germanic dress, but the Norman invaders brought fancy French fashions with them. These were quickly subverted in England. Floor-length French gowns were slit up the sides by English prostitutes to show off their legs and special pockets were made at the front to accommodate and accentuate the breasts.

By the fourteenth century, Geoffrey Chaucer was complaining of the 'scantness' of the hose which exposed the 'shamefull privy member of man' and made the buttocks behind 'the sheape of the full of the moon'. By the sixteenth century, the codpiece was added, which covered the genitals – or, more accurately, drew attention to them. At that time it was fashionable to sleep naked, even in Scotland. When James I of England, James VI of Scotland, was still a child and under the care of Lady Marr, he was taken ill one night with colic. All the male and female servants who ran to his assistance were naked, except for the countess herself, who wore a half-length shirt.

Bare breasts

When James I came to the throne of England, he introduced sumptuous new fashions. However, he also passed an Act that required young women to be seen in public with their breasts exposed to the nipple. This was seen as a symbol of their virginity at the time. In the court of his grandson Charles II, women who were far from virginal also exposed their necks, shoulders, arms and breasts. This was widely condemned.

In 1672, the book *New Instructions as to their Behaviour, together with a Discussion of some Novelties in the Mode; against powdering Hair, Naked Breasts and Patches, and other unseemly* Customs was published. This thoughtfully provided two illustrations demonstrating what the author was getting at. The first showed a woman with her breasts covered. It was captioned 'Virtue'. The other, bearing the caption 'Vice', showed her topless.

In 1678, Edward Cooke published *A just and seasonable Reprehension of naked Breasts and Shoulders Written by a Grave and Learned Papist*, with an introduction by the foremost theologian Richard Baxter. The book said it was bad enough that, at 'balls, in chambers of entertainment and in the walks, woman appear with naked breasts', but they also turned up to church half naked. It was enough to put one off one's prayers.

Padding

At the beginning of the eighteenth century, it was considered that the lower parts of women's bodies were too big, so fashions tried to make hips and buttocks look smaller. But by the middle of the century it was thought that the lower parts were too small, so fashions tried to make them look big. Then, in 1759 and 1760, the fashion was for all women, both young and old, to look as if they were pregnant. This was achieved by artificial stomachs made out of tin called 'pads' or 'paddies'. Men responded by wearing false calves.

Meanwhile necklines were bouncing up and down. At the beginning of the eighteenth century, it was considered indecent if two inches of flesh was seen below the neck. By the middle of the century the shoulders and much of the breasts were exposed again. Then women were muffled up to the chin, and then, in the 1770s, the shoulders and breasts were on display again.

Sex sells

In 1765, shopkeepers, particularly those in London's Bond Street, began hiring good-looking young men to serve their female customers, while men were encouraged to part with their money by pretty young shop girls and modistes, who often doubled as prostitutes, servicing the young dandies who frequented their stores. Women customers responded by committing adultery with rich and generous gentlemen to pay for the latest fashions.

Spanking fashions

Ever wondered what to wear to a flogging? *The Exhibition of Female Flagellants* insisted that 'Nakedness must be partial during flagellation in order to obtain the highest degree of satisfaction.' The book *The Romance of Chastisement* called this 'bath-nakedness', recommending the uncovering of the part that afforded greatest pleasure. The book condemns full nudity as improper, except when it is children who are being beaten.

In *The Merry Order of St Bridget*, there is a passive flagellant who requires that the woman who beats him be dressed as a nun. *The Romance of Chastisement* talks of governesses dressed in Empire costume, while in *The Sublime of Flagellation* they wear full gala costumes.

And the bride wore ...

In old England it was believed that, if a woman married in a state of undress, her new husband would not be responsible for her debts. The Fleet registers record a bride running across Ludgate Hill in her shift, and the *Daily Journal* of 8 November 1725 mentions a similar event in Ulcombe, Kent. In White-haven in 1766, a woman was married in church wearing nothing but a shift.

Others went further. In Grimsby, on 23 August 1815, a widow who wanted to ensure that her second husband would not be burdened with the debts of her first 'proceeded out of the window in a state of nudity, where she was received into the arms of her intended, in the presence of two substantial witnesses'.

The practice spread to America, where a widow remarrying was obliged to leave everything, including her clothes, to the creditors of her deceased husband. These nude weddings took place in the evening, when the light was low, or the naked bride stood in a recess, behind a curtain, or in a closet during the ceremony.

The fashion for nakedness

In 1794, the Directoire fashions came in from Paris, where those who had survived the Reign of Terror that followed the French Revolution were determined to have a good time. Parisians attended balls with their hair cropped or pinned up and a thick red ribbon around their necks as a humorous ref-erence to those who had been guillotined. Everyone was eager for sex – as an affirmation of life – and women's clothes became as revealing as possible. Josèphine de Beauharnais – later Bonaparte – whose first husband perished in the terror, danced naked in public with her friends, while Madame Hamelin was seen walking down the Champs-Elysées naked to the waist.

The 'fashion for nakedness' soon caught on in England. One of the champions of the fashion, Lady Campbell, appeared wearing a veil of transparent muslin and nothing else, and, though the bust had been seen in public before, now everything else was on show. Dire consequences were bound to ensue.

'When a cutting north-east wind blows,' said an eyewitness, 'cold, illness and death are brought with the sharp air to the thinly clothed bodies; the beauties shiver with cold, but fashion will have it not otherwise, and doctors, chemists and gravediggers reckon on a good harvest.'

The 'fashion for nakedness' then spread to men, who took to wearing flesh-coloured ballet tights, or skin-tight, flesh-coloured breeches and stockings, which made it look, from a distance, as if they were wearing a coat and shoes and nothing else.

Nipple rings

Although the 'aesthetic' and 'dress reform' movements of the 1880 sought to restrain extravagance in fashion, the English periodical *Society* in 1899 reported that women were having their nipples pierced and gold 'breast rings' set with brilliants inserted. This was done for purely erotic purposes and décolletage plunged to show them off.

An Oxford Street modiste, who had plainly seen a lot of

them in her line of work, wrote to *Society* about the fashion, saying she could at first not understand the trend for such a painful operation, but soon realised that 'many ladies are ready to bear the passing pain for the sake of love' and she 'found that the breasts of the ladies who wore rings were incomparably rounder and more fully developed that those who did not ...' So she had her own nipples pierced and rings inserted.

Society then went into the history of nipple piercing in loving detail. Apparently it dated back to the ancient Egyptians and the magazine thoughtfully included historic scenes of flagellation, in which naked girls were tethered to whipping posts by their nipple rings. The new fashion may be painful, the magazine said, but not as painful as the vogue among Abyssinian women, who had their breasts stung by bees until they swelled to three or four times their natural size.

A public boob

'It has recently been the fashion amongst the women of the world to appear half naked,' wrote a German visitor, 'and to display the hidden charms of their bodies, and quite a number of these fashionable females who have no natural bosom to display take refuge in artificial ones made of wax, so that they shall not be given away by the mode.'

However, false breasts have their pitfalls. In *The School for Fashion* (1800), the author, Madame Thicknesse, related a true story of how a woman who was about to be married fainted at a party and a number of women 'eagerly flew to her assistance, and upon loosening her gown to give her more air, out tumbled a pair of beautiful wax breasts on the floor!!'

Buying a divorce

In the early nineteenth century, ladies who did not need a boob job bought a device called a 'divorce'. It was 'designed, most unnaturally, to separate what the hand of the Creator had brought into the most graceful union … a piece of steel or iron, of a triangular form, gently curved on either side … covered with soft material … placed at the centre of the chest to divide the breasts'. The idea was to push the breasts apart to prevent the appearance of a cleavage.

Drawers on

In old England women's garments were frequently cumbersome and difficult to remove. Indeed upper-class women were unable to dress and undress without the help of a maid. This did not mean they were sexually unavailable, though. Until drawers became fashionable in the second decade of the nineteenth century, women's underclothes consisted of a light shift and stocking secured above the knee by coloured garters and no knickers – offering a lover unimpeded access if he simply raised her skirts and petticoats.

Public indecency

One of the reasons woman wore long skirts in old England was that they had no drawers on. Even so, being knickerless could have embarrassing consequences at key moments in your life. In 1752, Mary Blandy was about to be hanged publicly for poisoning her father when she cried out on the scaffold, 'Gentlemen, don't hang me high for the sake of decency.' Unfortunately for Mary, her modestly was not preserved after death. After she was cut down and taken to a nearby house where her coffin awaited, she was 'carried through the crowd upon the shoulders of a man with her legs exposed very indecently'.

The fires of love

During Britain's periodic fits of piety, it was thought indecent for people to strip off completely, even for sex. Some Puritanical husbands wore a long nightshirt called a chemise carouse, which had a strategic opening. This allowed procreation but hardly a glimpse or a feel of the naked flesh beneath.

A couple could go through their entire married life without seeing each other in the altogether. So much mirth was provoked when the story circulated of an eminent citizen of Edinburgh named John Jolly who, one night while making love to his wife, wanted to see her pudendum. But he dropped the candle and set fire to her pubic hair.

CHAPTER NINETEEN

Erotic Entertainments

 N OLD ENGLAND, entertainment usually involved excessive drinking. Then there was dancing and the theatre. And always not far beneath the surface there was an element of the erotic.

Lewd dancing

'Love dances' are mentioned in the works of Chaucer. These were performed by two nearly naked girls who struck erotic poses to show off their physical charms, and seemed to come on to each other. It appears to have its roots in the first Crusade, when knights brought Arab dancing girls back to England with them.

From the twelfth century until about 1530, young men and women in London were encouraged to dance outdoors on St Valentine's day to prevent them from doing 'worse things indoors'.

Kissing dances

In *Henry VIII*, Shakespeare mentions a kissing dance, which was common in England. One of the women dancers placed a cushion on the floor and selected a partner by reciting a rhyme. She then knelt on the cushion and was kissed by the male. Then she repeated the process, which continued until all of the dancers had been kissed.

In 1711, Joseph Addison, writing in the *Spectator*, complained of a kissing dance in which men and women kept their lips pressed together for a whole minute. He also complained of the allemande, in which dancers rolled on the floor making it possible to 'see far higher above the girl's shoes than was seemly'.

Magistrate Sir John Fielding – brother of the novelist Henry Fielding – complained that the private classes held by dancing masters were, in fact, orgies. And in the nineteenth century erotic balls were held upstairs at an exclusive brothel in Brompton run by Nellie Cawsten, attended by 150 'pretty ladies'.

Taverns

In his book *Le Pornographe*, published in Brussels in 1879, author Rétif de la Bretonne said that London could close its brothels, because the taverns performed the same function just as well.

'Both sexes meet without supervision,' he wrote, 'and those who have a lively inclination to pleasure can command agreeable satisfaction in a manner which cannot be found so easily anywhere else.'

Taverns had become the centre of sexual activity after the Restoration and remained so into the Georgian era. After visiting London in 1760s, Casanova said, 'I went for distraction to the Shakespeare Tavern. Lord Pembroke had told me that I should find the most beautiful women and the most agreeable virtue in the capital there.'

The Weatherby tavern was known as a meeting place for 'a great number of daughters of Venus of all classes, from the kept mistress to the common prostitute'. A tavern run by one Bob Derry was even known as the 'School of Venus', while the Golden Lion in the Strand was another well-known haunt of prostitutes and was, unsurprisingly, known as the 'Cat'.

Plyers to the tavern

In *The Adventures of a Speculist; or a journey through London* (1788), George Alexander Stevens called the prostitutes who conducted their business from the inns as 'plyers to the tavern' and explained how the system worked.

If guests did not mention women, the waiters, after the guests had had a few drinks, would tell them 'that four or five beautiful young women have stopped in chairs to ask after their honours, and left word that they'll call again; upon which an order is immediately dispatched to the bar, to signify, that when such and such ladies called again they are to be shewn up'.

In fact, the women had not stopped by in chairs, nor had they gone away. They were 'waiting shut up in a little room (like too many sheep penned up in Smithfield) to be sent for'.

Long rooms

In the nineteenth century, the London Society for the Protection of Young Females and Prevention of Juvenile Prostitution reported that prostitutes congregated in large numbers in the taverns.

'Fashionable and wealthy young men visited these places, and chose their mistress from those assembled,' the report said, adding,

> These saloons are attached to 'taverns', and are the source of much wealth. They were not exclusively confined to the West End of town, or London beyond Temple-bar. They are known in other parts under the name of 'long rooms', particularly along the banks of the Thames, where sailors abound. Some of these long rooms can accommodate five hundred persons.

Prostitutes were arranged like cattle waiting to be selected by sailors and other visitors.

The suited then enter another capacious apartment in the establishment, and after every kind of revelry, drinking, and dancing, the poor Jack-tars proceed to brothels, where they are stupefied by poisoned drink, robbed, and either forced into the streets, dressed or undressed, or absolutely murdered by bullies, and then secretly made away with … The owners of these houses make an enormous property by sales of 'refreshments', and 'other articles', and they encourage prostitutes, by either treating them to food and drink, or by giving them money.

'Gin palaces' doubled as brothels and taverns had convenient offshoots called 'night houses'. Then there were the oyster houses and 'dining rooms' around Covent Garden and Drury Lane, which had signs in the windows saying simply BEDS. Restaurants around Leicester Square also served dinner in private rooms and a number of fairly fashionable brothels around the area that found favour among French visitors.

Coffeehouses

Eighteenth-century coffeehouses were mainly respectable places. Some developed into great institutions such as Lloyd's of London, the Stock Exchange and White's club in St James's. But there were others of a more dubious character. Casanova called the Prince of Orange coffeehouse the most 'infamous place in the capital'. It was opposite the King's Theatre and the singers and dancers from the Opera House frequented it. Casanova's natural inclination, it is said, 'led him to look to the stage door for amorous adventure'.

As modern cafés developed, they attracted prostitutes. In 1870, the Turkish Divan in the Haymarket vied with the Café de la Régence for the night-time trade. And you did not have to sell coffee. Hickson's cake shop in Piccadilly sold cooled soda water, which became fashionable in 1810. It was also a fashionable place for beautiful women to display themselves.

Tea gardens

By 1700 numerous dubious tea gardens had sprung up on St George's Field, an area on the south bank of the Thames, between Southwark and Lambeth. Beside them were a number of miserable huts that housed prostitutes. At the centre was the Dog and Duck, which had opened in 1643, where gentlemen could meet 'Drury misses' and their 'bullies'. It closed in 1812.

The Apollo Garden was opened in 1788 by Mr Clagget, who owned the Pantheon in Oxford Street. It was supposed to be a rival to the famous Vauxhall Gardens, but developed such a reputation for prostitution that guidebooks of the time say that hardly anyone of 'good standing' was to be seen there at all. It closed after a few seasons and the grounds were levelled.

Vauxhall Gardens

The Vauxhall Gardens, though maintaining a respectable veneer, were also a haunt of prostitutes. They operated discreetly, often wearing masks. On 27 July 1688, Pepys – a regular visitor – remarked, 'How coarse some young gallants from the town were. They go into the arbours where there is no man and ravish the women there.' Admission was a shilling (5p).

In 1759, there were complaints that prostitutes and their clients were making a noise like 'Cavalcanti's bloodhounds' in the bushes and men were accused of raping women in lonely spots. But still amorous activities went on. The *French Observer* of 1769 said, 'A great many small isolated bushes have been put there, which are convenient for lovers. These perhaps attract the English women the most.'

Casanova's confidant, the dissolute Lord Pembroke, offered Marianne Geneviève Augspurgher de Charpillon 20 guineas – £21 or £2,000 at today's prices – for 'a quarter-of-an-hour's conversation in an arbour'. Later she consented to walk among the trees with Casanova for nothing, provided he would go to see her every day. Then she bled him dry. But in October 1763, Vauxhall Gardens began to lose their charm for Casanova and Pembroke. According to the *London Chronicle*, when the proprietors applied to renew their licence, they had to promise that the 'dark walks' would be lit before it was granted.

The Ranelagh

Casanova had more success at the Ranelagh Rotunda across the river in Chelsea, though Marianne eventually dropped him there and went off with Lord Grosvenor, leaving Casanova broken-hearted. These gardens had been laid out in 1742 and were supposed to be a covered version of Vauxhall. The entrance fee was half a crown (12½p).

In those days there was a wooden bridge between Chelsea and Pimlico. Nearby was a romantic spot called 'Jenny's Whim', now built over by Victoria Station. And, not far away, 'May Fair' between Piccadilly and South Audley Street was the source of many bad scandals during the eighteenth century.

The Ranelagh closed in 1803 and was demolished two years later. The site is now part of Chelsea Hospital Gardens.

Gardens of Venus

At Islington there was a Temple of Flora in the Garden of Venus. The prostitutes on their way there 'paraded through the streets in high carriages, dressed as Amazons, accompanied by other girls, in similar costumes, who rode alongside'. Men had to pay an entrance fee to get into the gardens; women got in free.

Marylebone Gardens, between Devonshire and Beaumont Streets, were laid out in the seventeenth century and visited by Pepys in 1688. By the eighteenth century they had become so notorious that they were mentioned in the *Sérails de Londres*, a guidebook to London nightlife published in Paris. They were closed in 1778.

From 1700 to 1730, there was an entire amusement complex at Belsize House in Hampstead with gardens, a race course, a theatre and a dance hall, which was favoured by prostitutes, as far too much 'gallantry' and 'licence' went on there. To drum up trade, the gardens put on 'charity concerts' where young men who had, perhaps, attended in all innocence found themselves surrounded by prostitutes and their procuresses.

In 1757 an Act of Parliament required licences for places of entertainment, and any without a licence were deemed disorderly. And fines were imposed on those running them and anyone found in them could be seized. This eventually closed many of the pleasure gardens. Others were built over as London expanded.

Rochester's Sodom

The theatre offered all sorts of erotic opportunities, especially after women began appearing on stage with the Restoration. During the reign of Charles II, a play appeared that must, by a country mile, be the most obscene production ever on stage. It was called *Sodom, or the Quintessence of Debauchery* and was almost certainly written by the Earl of Rochester. He was well known for his lewd poetry, some of it so obscenely satirical that he was repeatedly banished from court.

Rochester himself denied writing the play in a poem called

'To The Author of a Play Call'd Sodom', which matches the style of the drama so closely that even the most casual reader is led to assume he did. Rochester was, after all, a great prankster. It also closely matches his only acknowledged play, *Valentinian*.

In 1680, Rochester had a deathbed conversion and ordered 'all his profane and lewd writings' to be burned, and it was thought that play was lost. However, a version was published in Antwerp four years after his death.

Pisanus Fraxi, an expert in these matters, insists that *Sodom* had been performed before Charles II and his court. Women were banned from the performance, he says, but he assumed that they came in disguise as the prologue reads:

… I do presume there are no women here
't is too debauch'd for their fair sex I fear,
Sure they'll not in petticoats appear
And yet I'am inform'd, here's many a lass
Come for to ease the itching of her arse…

It gets worse.

The *dramatis personae* include:

BOLLOXIMIAN, King of Sodom

CUNTIGRATIA, Queen

PRICKETT, Young Prince

SWIVIA, Princess

BUGGERANTHUS, General of the Army

POCKENELLO, Pimp, Catamite, and the King's Favourite

BORASTUS, Buggermaster-general

PENE and TOOLY, Two Pimps of Honour

LADY OFFICINA, She-pimp of Honour

FUCKADILLA, CUNTICULA and CLITORIS, Maids of Honour

VIRTUOSO, Merkin and Dildo-maker to the Royal Family

FLUX, Physician to the King

With Boys, Rogues, Pimps, Caterpillars and other Attendants.

In Act I, the curtain rises on a room hung with obscene pictures and the King of Sodom issues a proclamation giving his subjects full sexual licence, unrestricted by law. As he is bored with having sex with the Queen and his other mistresses have other lovers, the King is persuaded to try pederasty with his courtiers. The Queen, it transpires, has already taken a lover. But under the circumstances, the King can hardly object.

Act II opens in a garden decorated with statues of naked men and women in various postures. In the middle, there is a fountain in the form of a woman standing on her head, with the spout of water issuing from between her legs. The Queen enters with three maids of honour, who complain that the King is neglecting them sexually and they discuss the sexual attributes of the other men of the court.

In the next scene, the Queen has sex with Lady Officina in the chair of state while the other maids of honour satisfy themselves with their dildos. The Queen then says that she wants a man. The scene concludes with an obscene song, while six naked men and women do a dance that involves cunnilingus and fellatio. Then they all have sex.

In the third act, the Prince and Princess commit incest, then Cunticula, a maid of honour, arrives and joins in. As a result the exhausted prince has to be confined to his bed.

In Act IV, the Queen tests the virility of General Bugger-anthus. Impressed, she wants to test it again, and again – until he is incapable. In a monologue the Queen then despairs at finding a man who can satisfy her. In the following scene, the King and his two male lovers discuss the advantages of ped-erasty – the King even saying that he now finds buggery with a turkey preferable to vaginal sex with a woman. A courtier enters and the King asks him how his proclamation has been received. When he is told that a woman has had sex with a stallion, the King orders an elephant to be put at her disposal. Then 20 boys sent by the King of Gomorrah turn up and the King has sex with one of them.

In Scene 1 of Act V, the maids of honour complain to the dildo maker that he is selling inferior goods, and demands that he make good with the real thing. When he gets it out, they are delighted with what they see, but in the event he becomes overexcited to the point where he is no use to them. In Scene 2, the action moves to another garden where the trees are the shape of phalluses. Men are playing dulcimers with their genitals while women play Jews' harps with theirs. The doctor, Flux, warns that the King's proclamation has resulted in anarchy. The Queen has died from overindulgence. The Prince has gonorrhoea and the Princess has been driven mad by the pain of the ulceration in her womb. The King asks whether anything can be done and Flux, the doctor, says:

To love and nature all their rights restore,
Fuck woman and let buggery be no more.
It doth the procreative end destroy,
Which nature gave with pleasure to enjoy.
Please her, and she'll be kind: if you displease,
She turns into corruption and disease.

That could have provided a nice moral ending for the play. But the King cannot bear the thought of going with a woman again and merely says,

I scorn the gift [of eternal life], I'll reign and bugger still.

Then demons and ghosts take to the stage and the King says to his catamites,

Let heaven descend, and set the world on fire –
We to some darker cavern will retire.
There on thy buggered arse I will expire.

At this point, the stage is engulfed with fire, brimstone, clouds of smoke and all the special effects the Carolean theatre can muster. But Rochester does not leave it at that. He has three epilogues spoken by Cunticula, Fuckadilla and Swivia that describe in the most graphic terms the pleasures of sex and their own sexual attributes. In fact, throughout the whole play there is hardly a line without the C-word or the F-word or one of the other words in the lexicon of lechery. You would not see anything half as filthy on a Dutch porn channel these days.

The Green Room

In Georgian times, actresses often supplemented their income by prostitution and used the stage as a form of advertising. *The Secret History of the Green Room* (1793) tells of their antics. One of the actresses' lives it records is that of Mrs Jordan.

When the Duke of Clarence (Prince William), son of George III, was 25 and an officer in the Royal Navy, he fell in love with the actress Dorothea Bland, who was five years his senior and went by the stage name of Mrs Jordan. She was the daughter of an Irish stagehand. At 20, she had had a child by Richard Daly, a Dublin theatre manager. Then she came to London, where she became an overnight success after appearing in Garrick's *The Country Girl*.

She soon became the mistress of the theatre owner, Sir Richard Ford, and made her name in 'breeches parts' – her long, shapely legs made her an ideal choice for playing the role of principal boy.

Dorothea was said to have 'fine animal spirits', but she also had a reputation for being vulgar and foul-mouthed – even by Regency standards. This was no problem for Prince William, who was often drunken and rowdy himself, and was said to have a sizable repertoire of salacious stories and jokes. Despite their obvious compatibility, however, he had to pursue Mrs Jordan for 11 months before he could brag to his brothers, 'You may safely congratulate me on my success.'

The Times confirmed this in a more cryptic fashion: 'That the Jordan has crossed the Ford is a matter no longer to be doubted, and the Royal Admiral has hoisted his flag.'

The couple settled down and began a family. Over the next 20 years, they had 10 children. But, as a bachelor prince, William had no money. So Mrs Jordan continued working to support their growing brood.

When she was 50 and had lost her figure, William abandoned her in the hope of marrying Miss Catherine Tylney-Long, who was considerably younger and heiress to a fortune worth £40,000 a year – over £2 million today. His callous behaviour drew widespread public condemnation.

Mrs Jordan was given a less than generous allowance and was told that she could keep her daughters, provided she did not return to the stage. Then she found herself landed with debts incurred by the son she had had by Richard Ford. She tried approaching William's brothers for help, but the royal family shunned her. So she was forced to give up her daughters and go back to acting. Then her health broke down and she had to flee abroad to escape her debts. Mrs Jordan eventually died completely penniless and quite alone in France.

The theatre didn't gain real respectability until Queen

Victoria came to the throne. Leading ladies became *haute bourgeois*, though lowly paid chorus girls and ballet dancers still sold themselves to supplement their wages.

Georgian theatres

The women plying their trade on the stage had to compete with the women in the auditorium. A German visitor in the early nineteenth century reported,

> The audience in the entire house – I am talking of Covent Garden and Drury Lane – is very mixed, and a duchess will often be found surrounded by prostitutes ... Indecent jokes are freely exchanged between these creatures and young men of the best families, and people do not appear to be in the least shocked even when the men make love to the prostitutes before their eyes.

Another visitor observed the scene at the Covent Garden Theatre.

> The saloon was full of prostitutes, whose clothes revealed more than they concealed, but whose behaviour, on the contrary, did not in any way betray their calling. A meaningful look from a man is answered by the lady concerned with the handing over of a card giving her name and address and containing a tenderly worded invitation. The girls carry the cards in their bosom, so they convey some of the perfume of their bodies.

Music halls

The music halls, showing variety acts, sprang up in the seventeenth century. But by the eighteenth century they were the haunts of prostitutes and they presented obscene burlesques on stage. Music-hall artistes frequently came up with smutty versions of popular songs, which were published in small booklets illustrated with suggestive drawings. *The Nobby Songster* of 1842 contained such classics as 'Miss Bounce of Cock Lane', 'A Young Flash Whore and an Old Jack Daw' and 'The Ladies' Tool'; and *Nancy Dawson's Cabinet of Choice Songs* that same year carried 'The Old Woman that Wants a Grind', 'That's About the Size of It', 'The Days We Went Rogering' and 'I Am the Stallion of the Town They Say'.

In the 1830s, prostitutes were heard singing obscene songs in the street to drum up trade. It was only in the 1870s that the music halls began to clean up their acts.

CHAPTER TWENTY

The Amorous Arts

 HROUGHOUT THE MIDDLE AGES, the only nudes in European art were Adam and Eve, suitably fig-leaved, and sinners being chastised in hell. The Renaissance changed all that. Suddenly the classical nude was back in fashion. Nudes even appeared on murals in churches and on altar pieces. But England was slow to catch up.

Erotic art

Erotic art in England began with illustrations to the great Italian poet Pietro Aretino's *Sonetti lussuriosi* – 'Lewd Sonnets' – made by Giulio Romano and the etchings made from them by Marc Antonio Raimondi. They showed 16 sexual positions. Despite the fact that the illustrations were suppressed, Aretino wrote some more sonnets and the number of sexual positions climbed to 36. Nearly all of Raimondi's original etchings were lost, but the last few copies were found during the storming of the Bastille in 1789.

Versions of the etchings began circulating in England in 1694. Students at All Souls College, Oxford, ran them off on the university press when the dean was away. Unfortunately, the dean returned early and confiscated the plates and a number of copies. However, 60 had already been disseminated. Although they were said to have been collected later and destroyed, illustrations of Aretino's positions soon appeared in London brothels.

Green fingers

In the eighteenth century, gardens were landscaped with artificial hollows and mounds, temples and columns in a clearly sexual way. These erotic gardens drew their inspiration both from the unparalleled sexual frankness of the time and the renewed interest in the classical culture of Greece and Rome.

The gardens at West Wycombe were laid out by Sir Francis Dashwood, founder of the Hell-Fire Club, in the shape of a naked woman. A frequent visitor, John Wilkes, an MP and mayor of London, wrote, 'There is one remarkable temple in the gardens at West Wycombe, dedicated to the Egyptian hieroglyphic for **** [sic]. To this object his lordship's devotion is undoubtedly sincere, though I believe now not fervent.'

At the centre of the gardens was the Mound of Venus. The grotto beneath the mound was known as Venus's Parlour and its entrance was called the Gate of Life. After Sir Francis's death, the Dashwood family called in Capability Brown to cover up the erotic symbolism, but lately the temple with the statue of Venus, which tops the Mound, has been restored. It has been said that Dashwood's erotic garden was a riposte to the nearby gardens at Stowe with its Temple of Ancient Virtue.

Interesting illustrations

Probably the first obscene pictures to be published in England were in the book *The Pleasures of Love: Containing a Variety of Entertaining Particulars and Curiosities in the Cabinet of Venus* (1755), which contained 16 erotic etchings. And in 1841 an illustrated version of John Cleland's 1749 erotic classic *Fanny Hill, or, Memoirs of a Woman of Pleasure* was printed.

The great cartoonist James Gilray drew scenes of flagellation, while Thomas Rowlandson's erotic drawings were published in 1872 in *Pretty Little Games for Young Ladies and Gentlemen. With Pictures of Good Old English Sport and Pastimes.* These were captioned with obscene verses. Among the sports and pastimes illustrated are a buxom maid mounting her beau in a garden called 'The Willing Fair, or any Way to Please', 'New Feats of Horsemanship', showing a man and

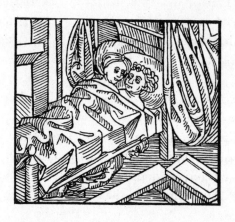

woman having sex on horseback at full gallop, and 'Rural Felicity, or Love in a Chaise', showing a couple at it in a coach while the woman whips the mount. 'The Hairy Prospect or the Devil in Fright' shows a girl raising her nightdress and putting the Devil to flight 'at the sight of a little pussy', and 'The Larking Cull' shows a well-endowed young man taking his beloved between the breasts. The British Museum has another 107 explicit and obscene Rowlandson etchings under lock and key.

Nipples in art

Before 1820, there were few female nudes in English painting. And whose there were followed the Continental model and had no pigmentation to their nipples or on areolae around them. This was because artists based their work not on nude models in the life class, but on the classical Greek and Roman sculptures unearthed during the Renaissance, which had long since lost their colouring. The man who overturned this fallacy was Yorkshire painter William Etty (1787–1849), who specialised in nudes. Though he never married, kept a mistress or, as far as is known, visited prostitutes, he gave the female nipple its rosy glow.

Etty was no libertine and his female nudes often have a flimsy piece of gauze covering their pubic region. However, in some cases the pudendum is revealed. He then painted pubic hair and other details of the female genitalia – a thing never done in classical antiquity, because female sexuality was considered too dangerous to depict.

No nudes

In the nineteenth century, the movement against the nude in art was far stronger in England than elsewhere. This resulted in the Pre-Raphaelite School of Art, which tried to capture a more spiritual eroticism. But, with the birth of photography, the floodgates were open. Initially, nude photographs were imported from France. Then, with the invention of halftone printing, a bunch of radical publishers got in on the act, using sales of erotica to subsidise their campaigning and pamphleteering.

When the widely anticipated British revolution failed to materialise, booksellers and printers found this former sideline had become too profitable to relinquish. Lubricious stories such as 'Lady Pokingham, or, They All Do it' (1881) and hard-core daguerreotypes, photographs and magic-lantern slides circulated widely. A huge business grew up in the book and paper shops around Leicester Square. Brothels decorated their reception rooms with pictures of naked women, each with a number so that a gentleman caller could make an informed choice. In the late nineteenth century, England sold more erotic photographs than any other country in the world.

Victorian pornography

The doyen of Victorian pornography was Henry Hayler. Beginning around 1870, Henry Hayler began producing his own nude photographs 'from life' and was soon doing business worldwide. On 31 March 1874, the police raided his studio, impounding more than 5,000 plates and 130,248 erotic photographs. Hayler fled to Berlin, then disappeared for good. Had he come to court he could scarcely have pleaded not guilty, since some of the pictures showed Hayler himself with his wife and two sons.

CHAPTER TWENTY-ONE

Lascivious Literature

T IS SAID THAT ENGLISH literature has produced only one great erotic classic – John Cleland's *Fanny Hill, or, Memoirs of a Woman of Pleasure* published in two volumes in 1748 and 1749. But it was not for the want of trying.

Criminal conversation

Although the Georgians and Victorians produced a huge amount of pornographic fiction, they had stiff competition from the real thing. According to the author of *London and Paris* of 1798, 'The most scandalous literature in London consists of the reports of the crim.-con. and divorce cases, which are printed without expurgation. No book is asked for so frequently in the lending library, and the editions, reprints and extracts from them prove their popularity.'

Later these became the stock-in-trade of the 'straw vendors'. When the selling of brochures and songs about 'criminal conversation' became illegal, vendors offered straw for sale, wrapped around an offending song. These were later sung or read aloud.

The Coal Hole

The theatre also cashed in on crim.-con. cases. Small theatres and touring companies were sure to draw a large audience with plays about adultery, and re-enactments of famous contemporary cases were staged frequently at the Coal Hole in the Strand.

A visitor to London in the 1870s wrote that the Cole Hole 'gives a dramatic, musical evening entertainment which has no precedent in any other place in the world and could have none'. Here, magistrates and jurymen were caricatured 'and propriety outraged'. He adds,

> A mock divorce trial is being performed. The opposing counsel call on witnesses who appear in the box one after the other in suitable costumes, amongst them many men dressed as women … The cross-examination to which they are subjected by the barrister or rather mock-barrister is extremely spicy! Licence has no limit here whatever. The judge finally sums up, puts a question to the jury, one of whom answers and passes sentence. Music follows and behind rises a curtain disclosing a brilliantly lighted little stage on which girls are grouped in flesh-coloured tights.

Dirty magazines

Erotic magazines began in England with the *Covent Garden Magazine, or Amorous Repository, calculated solely for the entertainment of the polite world* in 1774. It carried erotic poetry, lists of prostitutes and transcripts of scandalous law cases.

In 1783, the *Rambler's Magazine, or the Annals of Gallantry, Glee, Pleasure and the Bon Ton; calculated for the entertainment of the polite world; and to furnish the man of pleasure with a most delicious banquet of amorous, Bacchanalian, whimsical, humorous, theatrical and polite entertainment* appeared, packed with erotic stories. It went under in 1796, then reappeared in 1822. Another version ran from April 1824 to January 1825. Then the *Original Rambler's Magazine* appeared in 1827, this time with nudes in copperplate. Yet another *Rambler's Magazine* – sometimes known as the *New London Rambler's Magazine* – ran from 1827 to 1829.

The most fashionable of the Georgian lads' mags was the *Bon Ton Magazine; or Microscope of Fashion and Folly* which started in 1791, carrying erotic tales and copperplates. Then in 1795 came a magazine whose protracted title told you what it was about. It was called the *Ranger's Magazine, or the Man of Fashion's Companion; being the whim of the month and general assemblage of love, gallantry, wit, pleasure, harmony, mirth, glee and fancy. Containing a monthly list of the Covent Garden Cyprians; or a man of pleasure's vade mecum. The annals of gallantry. Essence of trials for adultery. Crim. Con. Seduction. Double entendres. Choice anecdotes. Warm narratives. Curious fragments. Animating histories of Tête-à-têtes, and wanton frolicks. To which is added the fashionable chit-chat and scandal of the month, from the Pharaoh Table to the Fan warehouse.*

In November 1830, the *Diurnal Register of the Freaks and Follies of the Present Day* – known informally as the *Crim.-Con. Gazette* – started, which later became the *Bon Ton Gazette* and added erotic poetry and memoirs to its reports of scandalous court cases. The *Quizzical Gazette* and *Merry Companion* ran from 27 August 1831 to 14 January 1832, when it closed despite its saucy woodcuts.

The Exquisite: a collection of Tales, Histories and Essays, funny, fanciful and facetious. Interspersed with anecdotes, original and select. Amorous adventures, piquant jests and spicey sayings, illustrated with numerous engravings began its weekly run in 1842. At just fourpence – just over £1 today – it carried erotic fiction and non-fiction, poems, letters on flagellation and articles on the cult of the phallus, along with articles translated from French and Italian.

The Pearl

The most obscene of all was *The Pearl, a monthly journal of facetiae and voluptuous reading* published in Oxford from July 1879 to December 1882. It carried erotic stories such as that old chestnut 'Lady Pokingham, or, They All Do it', 'Miss Coote's Confessions, or the voluptuous experiences of an old maid', which contains scenes of flagellation, 'La rose d'amour, or the adventures of a gentleman in search of pleasure', 'My Grand-mother's Tale, or May's account of her introduction to the art of love' and an erotic parody of Benjamin Disraeli's *Lothair*.

Each year *The Pearl* published a special supplement. In 1879, it was *Swivia, or the Briefless Barrister*, which was the story of an orgy between four men and two servants. It ran to 64 pages and was illustrated with five colour pictures.

The following year there was *The Haunted House, or the Unveiling of Theresa Terence*. Its 62 pages concentrated on flagellation and defloration. Christmas 1881 saw *New Year's Day, a sequel to Swivia, Vanessa and other tales* illustrated with six obscene coloured lithographs. It cost three guineas – £200 today. Then in 1882 came *The Erotic Casket Gift Book*, containing eight erotic tales left over from the demise of the magazine – surely the perfect Victorian stocking filler.

In August 1882, *The Cremorne* published 'Lady Hamilton, or Nelson's Inamorta: The Real Story of her Life', along with two obscene coloured lithographs and other erotic stories, all for one guinea. The following year saw the birth of *The Boudoir*, containing such tales as 'Voluptuous Confessions of a French Lady of Pleasure' and 'Adventures and Amours of a Barmaid' at 10s. 6d. – or £35 today.

The Private Case

During the nineteenth century, so much erotic literature was being published that in 1866 the British Museum Library began its 'Private Case' to store the collections of pornography bequeathed to it by Victorian gentlemen, including Henry Spencer Ashbee, the redoubtable Pisanus Fraxi himself. However, pornographic books from the collection of George III, the basis of the original library, also found their way into the Private Case.

The British Museum also kept other locked cupboards of books that did not appear in the main catalogue. These even included a special collection of books that had been banned by a court order and supposedly destroyed. There are around 2,000 volumes of erotica in the Private Case.

Many of the books mentioned elsewhere in this tome are kept in the Private Case under lock and key. And, to this day, they must be read on special desks in the reading room, not be left unattended and be returned half an hour before the library closes.

The Strange Laws of Old England

Nigel Cawthorne

Did you know that:

The law requiring a London taxi driver to carry a bale of hay on top of his cab to feed the horse was in force until 1976?

Under a Tudor law Welshmen are not allowed into the city of Chester after dark?

Under a statute of Edward II all whales washed up on the shore belong to the monarch?

Nigel Cawthorne takes you on an entertaining tour of the wilder shores of the British legal system as he unearths an extraordinary collection of the most bizarre and arcane laws that have been enacted over the centuries. Some of the laws, incredibly, are still in force. It is still illegal to enter the Houses of Parliament in a suit of armour...

This elegant and amusing book is perfect for everyone fascinated by the eccentric history of the British Isles.

978-0-74995036-1

The Curious Cures of Old England

Nigel Cawthorne

Another highly entertaining trawl through the byways of English history by the author of *The Strange Laws of Old England* and *The Sex Secrets of Old England*.

The history of medicine in Britain is full of the most bizarre cures for all manner of ailments, from the plague to the pox. A 16th century cure for dizziness was: Take a young swallow from her nest when the crescent moon is in Virgo; cut off the head and let the blood run into a vessel containing frankincense; then give it to the patient when the moon is waning.

But amidst all the eccentric – and sometimes lethal! – treatments there were some that, incredibly, seemed to work; and they form the basis of many of the medicines we know today.

978-0-7499-5072-9

The Lives of the English Rakes

Fergus Linnane

Rake: 'A loose, disorderly, vicious, wild, gay, thoughtless fellow; a man addicted to pleasure' Dr Johnson's Dictionary, 1755

The English Rake strides through the pages of romantic fiction, impossibly handsome, cynical and dangerous; a gambler, a deadly swordsman leaving a trail of broken hearts and slain rivals in his wake. The reality was, if anything, more intriguing. Some rakes were poets and playwrights of genius, including the dazzling Earl of Rochester, author of revered, tender lyrics but guilty of spectacularly debauched behaviour.

In this unique and entertaining book you will become intimately acquainted with those fascinating, colourful characters who have the dubious accolade of being the biggest rogues, lechers and profligates of history.

978-0-7499-5123-8